# FROM THE
# PRISON
## TO THE
# PALACE

**Publishing Details**

*From the Prison to the Palace* by Karen Roper
Published by Karen Roper © All rights reserved

The moral right of the author has been asserted. All rights reserved. Without limiting the rights under copyright restricted above, no part of this publication may be reproduced, stored in or introduced into a retrieval system, or transmitted, in any form or by any means (electronic, mechanical, photocopying, recording or otherwise), without the prior written permission of the copyright owner of this book. The views of the author belong solely to the author and are not necessarily those of the publisher or the publishing service provider.

1st Edition 2024, pbk.
ISBN: 978-0-6455581-2-8 (Paperback)
ISBN: 978-0-6455581-3-5 (ebook)

**Publishing services by:** PublishMyBook.Online
A catalogue record for this book is available from the National Library of Australia.

www.livingthelifegodintended.com
Most quotations (except where stated) from the Bible are from the Spirit Filled Life Bible Copyright © 1991 by Thomas Nelson, Inc.

# FROM THE PRISON TO THE PALACE

## A JOURNEY OF EMOTIONAL HEALING

### KAREN ROPER

# TABLE OF CONTENTS

| | |
|---|---|
| Prologue | vii |
| Chapter 1: What Put Us in the Prison? | 1 |
| Chapter 2: Joseph's Early Life | 13 |
| Chapter 3: Joseph's Early Life in Egypt | 29 |
| Chapter 4: Prison of Insecurity | 45 |
| Chapter 5: Prison of Doubt | 63 |
| Chapter 6: The Prison of Missing the Mark | 79 |
| Chapter 7: Rejection | 95 |
| Chapter 8: Prison of Shame | 111 |
| Chapter 9: Joseph in the Palace | 127 |
| Chapter 10: Forgiveness | 143 |
| Chapter 11: Restoration | 155 |
| Chapter 12: Peace | 165 |
| Chapter 13: Plan of God | 181 |
| Chapter 14: Eternal Perspective | 195 |
| Epilogue | 205 |
| Want to know Jesus | 209 |

# PROLOGUE

The day I was born was not an eventful one—it was not a world-changing event or even a public holiday. However, it was the day my journey started.

Most babies are born into a loving family of two parents—dad and mum, and maybe a few brothers and/or sisters. It is a joyous occasion for the family as they welcome their newborn. The labour might have been hard, but it is all soon forgotten in the joy of the new baby.

My beginning was not like that. I was never wanted by my birth mother. Her parents did not even know I was soon to exist. I am not sure what my birth father's feelings were; he already had three children with another woman. I was born and then left in a hospital with no one to care for me except for the nurses who were on that shift.

My name (identity) was changed three times in that first month of life. My birth mother called me Sharon, the nurses called me Helen and finally, my adoptive parents named me Karen.

Even though I was adopted out at one month old, the feelings of rejection, abandonment and insecurity began in my life on the day of my birth. It was further compounded by the change of my identity in the first month of my life. It was many years before I realised that God totally loved me, totally planned for my existence, totally had a new identity in Him for me and totally had an amazing plan for my life.

It is out of that that this book is written. However, it is not my life story that I will be sharing but Joseph's from the Bible as we can learn much as we delve into the emotions behind his story.

This book is the next one in the series and although we are going to navigate through the life of Joseph, it is not a long story but the journey that he took is one that most of us will face on our Christian walk.

In this book, I want to concentrate on the emotions of Joseph and the character traits that might have shaped his life. I am going to take some poetic licence and imagine what he might have gone through at the different stages of his life. This will assist us in seeing what can happen in our lives and how God can set us free from circumstances not always in our control.

This journey is not for the faint-hearted. It may be a painful journey, but it is worth it. The journey involves looking deep within ourselves to ensure nothing is holding us back from claiming our rightful place in the palace. We may have given our lives to Jesus, but we still might not be free.

This book will assist by setting us free from prisons that have held us back and then resetting our lives in the light of what Jesus did for us on the cross. Most of us don't want to get stuck in our prisons but want to take that journey through to the palace, which represents the Kingdom of God. If you are unsure of taking the steps you need, have a friend or relative go through this book with you. You may also require a trained counsellor to assist you through the painful areas of your life that need healing so you can live free.

I have been on this journey many times in my life as I have either put myself or someone put me in the prison of self-doubt, insecurity, rejection, not feeling good enough, etc., for too many years. Now that I know that I am a princess of God and belong in that new Kingdom, my life has forever changed.

Maybe you find yourself in a real prison. I hope that this book will allow you to see the potential for change. It will allow you to see none of us, including you, were created for a prison but were always created to live in a palace—the Kingdom of God here on earth and then forever in eternity.

Let's pray:

> *Father, as we start this journey of uncovering those things deep within us that need to be healed, I pray that not only will you reveal those hidden things but will hold our hands through this journey. We know God that you will never leave us or forsake us, but we want to feel You close as we undertake the journey to be free. In Jesus' name, amen.*

CHAPTER 1

# WHAT PUT US IN THE PRISON?

My question to all of us at the start is: are we in a prison? This may be a strange question to ask right at the start. However, it is a necessary question. For healing to begin, we must recognise where we are at.

We must look at and know the state of our flocks as it states in Proverbs 27:23. The next part of that verse states that we need to put our heart into caring for our herds.

If we don't recognise where we currently are, we won't know the path to take. I have been on a few bushwalks and it is hard to know where you are up to if you haven't been there before.

My husband and I do one bushwalk that's easy and is situated around half an hour from our home. We have walked the track many times and basically know where we are up to. We know where the fork in the path is, where we can take a detour or walk the long way around. But if we were on an unfamiliar track and there was no map, then we wouldn't know where to go.

We need to look within ourselves and be honest. Sometimes, it helps to look at our external reactions to situations. I know we can lash out at others if we don't feel secure within ourselves, especially if we think we are missing out.

Have you noticed reactions to things in your own life that are telling a deeper story? Is there something in your past that someone has done or has just happened, holding you back from everything that God has for you?

Could it be that we are bound in some sort of prison, either literally or in ourselves?

Most of us think of a prison as somewhere where people are put who have disobeyed the laws of the land. That is one definition of a prison. I want to explore the fact that there is another sort of prison. It's not physical but touches us in the soul—that area of the mind, will and emotions.

Some of us can tamp down that prison and give an outward appearance that it doesn't exist for us. However, I think that there is a prison in each of our souls (unless we have been totally healed by God).

In the Merriam-Webster Dictionary, 'prison' means a state of confinement or captivity. This is where we all find ourselves just before the start of our salvation walk before we accept Jesus as our Lord and Saviour.

But even after that, we can still be held captive by things that happened in our past or were said about us. Jesus restores our spirits but as Romans 12:2 states that we must renew our minds.

Faith is the language of God and fear is the language of Satan. Fear is the root of the prisons we find ourselves in.

So how did it start? Was it always meant to be this way? Didn't God create the earth good? Why are we still battling with this?

For the answers to all those questions, let's start reading in Genesis 1.

In Genesis 1:26–28, it states:

> *Then God said, "Let Us make man in Our image, according to Our likeness; let them have dominion over the fish of the sea, over the birds of the air, and over the cattle, over all the earth and over every creeping thing that creeps on the earth."*
>
> *So, God created man in His own image; in the image of God, he created him; male and female He created them.*
>
> *Then God blessed them, and God said to them, "Be fruitful and multiply; fill the earth and subdue it; have dominion over the fish of the sea, over the birds of the air, and over every living thing that moves on the earth".*

In verse 31, it states:

> *Then God saw everything that He had made, and indeed it was very good. So, the evening and the morning were the sixth day.*

God created mankind perfect and good. There was no confinement or captivity involved. Mankind was given dominion over all the animals of the earth. The plants and trees were given for mankind and the animals to eat. There was no fear, just an order of dominion.

In the *Strong's Exhaustive Concordance* of the Bible, 'prison' is the word *radah* in Hebrew and means to prevail against, reign or rule.

Adam and Eve (later) were to rule over the animals, but the animals had no fear of them. There was no confinement or captivity involved.

What changed the world to bring fear in?

Genesis chapter 3 has the answer. This chapter is titled 'The Temptation and Fall of Man' but it really could be titled 'The Day that Fear First Ruled'.

Satan made a play for Eve first. He probably figured that since she was told the information regarding the tree of the knowledge of good and evil from Adam and not God, then maybe she didn't have a strong enough conviction.

In verse 1 of chapter 3, Satan asks Eve a question—"Has God indeed said, 'You shall not eat of every tree of the garden?'" What sort of question is this? One that comes to play in our minds too. Has God indeed said that your family will be saved? Has God indeed said that you will be totally healed? Has God indeed said that He will prosper you? Has God indeed said that He will protect you? Satan still has us questioning God and we need to be aware of this deception and cast it out.

Then the next bit of the question is 'you shall not eat of every tree', so what are you missing out on? This question is one that we all have to grapple with. It's the reason that we end up in captivity to addictions, low self-esteem, etc. because none of us really wants to miss out if the thing is good. Sometimes, we don't want to miss out even if the thing is bad. It's not the item that we grapple with, but the fear of missing out.

Eve takes the bait. She should have answered, 'I have plenty of trees to eat from as God has provided for us abundantly. There is only one tree out of all the thousands of trees around me and I am okay with that as I totally trust God.' If that had been her answer, our lives could have been different.

But in verse 3, she answered that she couldn't eat that tree or touch it as God said. God never said they couldn't touch it only that they couldn't eat its fruit. The way that Eve said what God said reminds me of my children when they said to their friends, 'Mum said we can't go.' They may never have asked me for permission in some cases, as they just didn't want to go. But rather than saying 'no' and taking responsibility, they blamed the authority figure instead. Do you find yourself doing this too? We blame our boss, our spouse, our teachers, our pastor, etc. Don't blame, as you will ruin the relationship.

By putting the responsibility for the command back on God, she missed the point of relationship. God wanted and desired a relationship with Adam and Eve. He didn't want a garden full of robots.

Relationship will always produce a responsibility from the person being questioned but 'prison' blames somebody else. Eve blamed God because she couldn't eat from that tree.

This conversation wasn't going well and got a lot worse. Eve also said if they ate of the tree they would die, which was correct. I wonder if she really knew what 'die' meant.

Satan said, 'You won't die but you will be like God' in verses 4 and 5. Haven't we heard this before in our lives? *It's okay if you have the drug. You won't die but you'll feel euphoric. Nothing else is going to give you that high. It's okay if you have the first drink. You need to numb your pain and then you won't have to deal with it. It's okay if you feel that way about that person. There are no consequences if you say the wrong thing to them.* These types of thoughts and actions can lead to a place we never meant to go.

In verse 6, Eve takes the fruit and eats it for three reasons that have nothing to do with hunger. They are:

- It was good for food
- It was pleasant to the eyes
- It was desirable to make one wise

Let's look at these three things individually to see how we can get stuck in 'prisons' in our souls.

## It was good for food

Even though Eve wasn't hungry, there was a longing in her that needed to be satisfied. As Christians, our satisfaction should come from our relationship with God and if we feel empty, we need to check our God tank. Are we satisfying ourselves with the love and presence of God or has that become so familiar to us that we are starting to crave other things?

Psalm 42:1–5 should be our go-to psalm when we are feeling like our yearning for God is starting to dry up. It states:

> *As the deer pants for the water brooks, So pants my soul for You, O God. My soul thirsts for God, for the living God. When shall I come and appear before God? My tears have been my food day and night, while they continually say to me, where is your God?*
>
> *When I remember these things, I pour out my soul within me. For I used to go with the multitude; I went with them to the house of God. With the voice of joy and praise, with a multitude that kept a pilgrim feast.*
>
> *Why are you cast down, O my soul? And why are you disquieted within me? Hope in God, for I shall yet praise Him for the help of his countenance.*

We need to get our satisfaction from God and not from what this world has to offer. That is where we need to keep our eyes directed—on God.

## It was pleasant to the eyes

How many times have we looked at something and longed for it even though we know that it is bad for us? For example, that extra bit of cake, that third alcoholic drink, that cigarette, that magazine that is filled with pornography, etc.

Sometimes social situations can allow us to form prisons in our lives, like that group of popular teens that we long to join but shame and rejection comes over us when they tell us they don't want us.

All our friends are going to a nightclub or bar on a Friday or Saturday night, and we feel like a nobody because they didn't invite us and if they did, we probably wouldn't go anyway.

That boyfriend/ girlfriend situation where everyone is pairing up and not doing God's will and we feel lonely because we don't have a partner.

These are all things we see with our eyes that can allow prisons to develop in our lives. God loves us unconditionally and He wants us to see ourselves the way He sees us. He wants us to enjoy His creation: the beach, the mountains, the country and the city, and everything good in them. What He doesn't want is for us to look around and find ourselves coming up short.

We need to look to Jesus because He will tell us the truth about us: we are loved, accepted, a prince/princess of the

King, redeemed, uniquely created and with a purpose that is far beyond what we can see.

Let's look to Jesus to receive what He has for us and not this world that shows us good times but doesn't show us the consequences.

I remember a time in my life when I felt left out because I didn't have a boyfriend. So I went looking in the wrong circles. The consequence of that decision still has ramifications to this day. I ended up being pregnant outside of marriage (I absolutely love and adore my son—he has taught me so many things and my life would be poorer without him in it) and suffering in an abusive relationship before God intervened and enabled me to find my way out. But it was a high price to pay for not waiting on God for His best for me.

## It was desirable to make one wise

Things that are not of God will never make us wise. Wisdom is only found in God as He is the creator of all things and knows how everything works.

When we walk in our own wisdom, we are saying that we are much smarter than everybody else and don't need anybody in our corner, including God.

1 Corinthians 3:18–21b states:

> *Let no one deceive himself. If anyone among you seems to be wise in this age, let him become a fool that he may become wise. For the wisdom of this world is*

> *foolishness with God. For it is written,*
> *"He catches the wise in their own craftiness", and*
> *again, "The Lord knows the thoughts of the wise, that*
> *they are futile". Therefore let no one boast in men.*

God's ways and wisdom are so much higher than ours. This is why we should seek His wisdom as James 1:5 states.

We put ourselves in a prison when we don't go to God for wisdom. Some of us put ourselves down and say we are not smart or will never amount to anything. Others of us boast about how many degrees we have and the pay packet we earn.

But none of this matters when we seek God. God gave us each unique talents so there should be no comparison. God also told us in 1 Corinthians 12 that just like our own physical body is made up of many parts, so is God's body of believers on Earth.

Some of us have talents that can be physically seen like our own arms and legs. Others have hidden talents like the heart and lungs of our body that cannot be seen but are vital for the body of Christ to be alive.

Seek the wisdom of God and not your own or someone else's wisdom. Note—a person may speak the wisdom of God to you and that's okay.

Back to our story in Genesis. Eve ate the fruit and so did Adam and the prison and bondage of each person's life began.

In verse 7 of Genesis 3, once they ate the fruit, their eyes were opened and they knew they were naked so they covered themselves. A prison of any sort will work the same in our lives. There is a naked part of us that we don't want others to see so we hide it.

How do we do this? Some people do it through humour, others through shyness and others through being the life of the party. But all those things and more are our ways to cover up the things in our lives that we don't want to be uncovered.

I pray this book will help us all to expose those things in our lives and receive the healing that we need. God doesn't want us to walk in bondage but freedom.

Adam and Eve even hid from God. Sometimes the prisons we find ourselves in will cause us to hide either our whole selves or a part of our lives from God. But don't think for a minute that will succeed as God already knows and loves us anyway.

Prisons will also cause us to blame others for our demise. This can be seen in our story from verses 12 to 19. Adam blamed Eve and Eve blamed the snake. We do the same. We blame our childhood, our family, our social status, our economic status, the words spoken over us, our lack of a father/mother or the authority figures in our lives.

Blaming is not going to get us healed from our prisons. All blaming does is give power to the circumstances/people that caused our prison and none of us wants that. We need to expose those things by taking responsibility and getting healing.

God gave severe consequences to Adam and Eve for choosing to not obey Him. The choices we make in the three areas above also have consequences that are hard if we aren't obeying God.

One note—people may appear to have it altogether on the outside but it is on the inside (the hidden part) where prisons occur. Don't look at others or compare yourselves to them because everyone has a prison that they need to be freed from.

This book will provide freedom from that prison and the healing that we all need.

Let's pray:

*Father, we come to you and ask that as we read this book, you will expose those areas in our lives where we are bound as in a prison. I pray your healing power will be present throughout this book to provide the healing that we all need. We are ready and open for you to impart your wisdom in these areas. Amen.*

CHAPTER 2

# JOSEPH'S EARLY LIFE

To continue on our journey from the prison to the palace, we are going to look at Joseph's story in Genesis. I am going to take poetic licence through some of it as the Bible is not very clear on the emotions he may have gone through in each stage of his journey. The only emotion we see from him is when he cries when he is reunited with his brothers. But surely Joseph must have experienced other emotions too. Let's take a look!

We will go a little way back in Joseph's family history. His great-grandfather was Abraham, who was married to Sarah. He was the one whom God called to leave everything—his country, his family and his livelihood—and follow God to a place where he had never been before. Abraham is known as the father of faith and is the person whose story we read when we need to see a practical example of walking by faith.

He had one son of the flesh (his own desire) who was Ishmael, and one son of promise (a promise from God) who was Isaac, whose family line we need to follow to get to Joseph.

Isaac had two sons—Esau and Jacob. Jacob's name meant deceiver and that is who he was until God met him and changed his name to Israel. When we read the stories of Abraham and later, Isaac, we see that they each deceived the king of one of the nations into believing their wife was their sister. In fact, Abraham did this twice (once when he was still known as Abram (Genesis 12) and later when he was known as Abraham (Genesis 20)). This deception was carried on down through the generations and became more of a stumbling block as each generation passed. We will talk more about that later.

Jacob had two wives—Leah (who was given to him through her father's deception) and Rachel (whom Jacob really loved). He also fathered children through his two wives' maids, Zilpah and Bilhah.

The first children to be born were from the union of Jacob and Leah and their names were:

1. Reuben
2. Simeon
3. Levi
4. Judah

In Genesis 30:1, we start to see the jealousy coming through that would later be the downfall of Joseph and it came from his mother. Rachel was barren and she demanded that Jacob give her children. I am not sure where he could have produced them from but Rachel's jealousy of her sister caused a dissension.

So Rachel decided the best thing to do would be to allow her maid to be in union with Jacob. It sounds startlingly familiar to the story of Abraham and Sarah (his grandfather) when Sarah gave her maid to Abraham so she could have a child. It did not end well as it was totally out of the will of God.

The children born of the union of Jacob and Bilhah were:

1. Dan
2. Naphtali

Jealousy again prevailed and when Leah realised she wasn't bearing any more children, she did the same as Rachel and gave her maid to Jacob.

The children born of the union of Jacob and Zilpah were:

1. Gad
2. Asher

Leah conceived her next child through stealth and deception (verses 14–19). This was not a happy family that Joseph would have been born into but one full of jealousy and deception.

The next children born of the union of Jacob and Leah were:

1. Issachar
2. Zebulun, and their sister Dinah.

In verse 22, God remembered Rachel and Joseph was born. His name means 'God has taken away my reproach'. In the *Oxford Dictionary*, 'reproach' means the expression of disapproval or disappointment.

Rachel had disapproval and disappointment as her constant companions as she could not bear children. Where was this coming from? Maybe from Leah, but Leah would have been gloating or boasting that she gave Jacob six sons so this feeling would not be coming from her. Leah neither disapproved nor was disappointed in Rachel. She was just proud of her achievements. The feelings would have come as a result of Leah's achievements but not because of them.

Sometimes this happens to us. We get jealous of someone else's achievements but that is only the surface feelings. Deep down inside of us, there is a prison we have created of insecurity, disappointment, rejection, etc. That is the real issue and one that needs to be dealt with. If that is the case in your life, we will look at these things later in the book.

Jacob, however, is silent on this issue but from his actions in the past, he neither disapproved nor was disappointed in Rachel. He was just glad he had two wives and children.

Oftentimes, what we are feeling is not what others think but what we think about ourselves as a result of others' actions. This is why the Bible tells us in Romans 12:2 in the NIV Bible that we need to be transformed by the renewing of our minds and not be conformed to the world we currently live in.

'Conformed' means we model the behaviour and actions and that is what we do in our minds. People speak negative words to us and we conform to that way of thinking about ourselves instead of rejecting those words.

Being transformed by the renewing of our minds means we need to be in the Word of God and not only reading it but doing it. We need to be saying over ourselves what God does. We are not a disappointment and He doesn't disapprove of us. He sent His only son to die for us so we could be reconciled to God. If God was disappointed in us or didn't approve of us, He would never have sent His Son.

Let's look at another quick story of a barren woman before we leave Rachel. The story is of Hannah in 1 Samuel 1. Hannah was also barren but her husband's comments to her in verse 8 are beautiful. He said, 'Am I not better to you than ten sons?' He was in essence telling her that he saw her pain, but he was not disappointed in her nor did he disapprove of her.

Unlike Rachel, Hannah did one thing that showed her heart. She went to the temple and cried out to God. Rachel never cried out to God (or if she did, the story isn't written). Hannah knew where her help would come from and that was

God. Both women's sons were destined for greatness, but Samuel had a God-fearing mother and Joseph didn't.

Getting back to the current story, Rachel would have been happy to finally have a son. She probably would have spoiled Joseph and as Jacob loved Rachel the most, he probably would have spoiled him too.

The other brothers would have seen this and resentment and jealousy would have started to grow. This can be the same in any family if the emotions of the children are not managed well. A new baby can take up a lot of time and for Rachel, the brothers would not have worried. But how much time did Jacob spend with this little one? He would have been older by now and most of the work would have fallen to his other sons. So maybe he was more of a doting father to Joseph than he was to the other sons because of this.

The last son to be born to Jacob was Benjamin in Genesis 35:16–20. But his birth was marred by tragedy as Rachel died giving birth to him. She called his name Ben-Oni, which means 'son of my sorrow', but Jacob changed it to Benjamin, which means 'son of my right hand'.

Rachel was still bitter regarding her circumstances but Jacob loved her regardless as he put a pillar on her grave for all to remember her by, which is still there to this day. You can visit this memorial site in Israel.

We don't know how old Joseph was at this time, possibly only a small boy. But the death of his mother would have had a major impact on his life.

In the book *Bereavement: Reactions, Consequences, and Care*, it suggests that:

> A major area of concern regarding psychological functioning following bereavement relates to negative shifts in self-concepts and self-esteem. Rochlin and Kliman have observed that children often assess themselves more negatively after a parent's death than before. Children who interpret a parent's death as desertion because the parent did not love them may believe that they are unlovable, which may result in a persistent sense of low self-esteem.
>
> Following a major relationship loss, a child may see himself as helpless and vulnerable. It is possible that this image of being frighteningly small and helpless is the most disruptive and disorganizing view of the self that can emerge subsequent to parental death.[1]

Although the Bible does not give us specifics about how Joseph handled his mother's death, based on what happened a few years later, we can see that the above research may be correct in Joseph's case. He would have had low self-esteem as

---

[1] https://www.ncbi.nlm.nih.gov/books/NBK217849/

his brothers probably rubbed it in that he had no mother. One of the other mothers may have had to become his substitute mother and they probably would have rebelled against it. They had their own children to attend to.

Joseph may have had to grow up fast and feel like he was responsible for his brother, Benjamin. This can lead to trying to be mature in an immature body and brain and not being able to handle the responsibility well.

The nature of this family being rooted in deception and jealousy probably would not have leant itself to being supportive of the young boys.

Another thing is that when Rachel died, they were in the midst of the journey from Laban's (Leah and Rachel's father) home back to the home of Isaac and Rebecca. This journey was not like it would have been today. There were no fast trains or planes to travel on but a slow trek with their animals and belongings through wilderness and desert.

The boys could not even go and visit their mother's grave as she was buried on the way and chances are, they would never return to that site. It was like they were told to forget her and get on with life. This would not have helped their grieving process at all and much would be carried over into their later lives.

Joseph also would have felt very protective of his new baby brother. He was the only full-blood relative that Joseph had and he may have taken on the responsibility for his brother, or tried to. The adults in his life would probably have chased him away.

We see then that from an early age, Joseph's life was marked by jealousy, grief, deception and a protectiveness of his brother. All these traits and possibly others not mentioned, formed who Joseph was in later life.

The one topic we haven't discussed is Joseph's relationship with God and how that came about.

All we know is that a few verses earlier in Genesis 35, God told Jacob to take his family up to Bethel (where he first made an altar) and Jacob advised his family to put away foreign gods, purify themselves and change their garments. Once they did this, then in verse 5, it states that the terror of God was upon the cities they passed through.

This would have also impacted Jacob's family, including the small boy, Joseph.

The next time Joseph is mentioned is in Genesis 37. He was now about 17 years old. As far as we know, none of the issues in his life had been dealt with but they were about to get far worse.

Joseph's job at this stage was as a shepherd. In verse 2, he was busy tending the flock with his brothers. It is interesting who the Bible says he was with. It was not with all his family, only Zilpah, Bilhah and their sons. Where were Leah and her sons? Maybe by now, her boys were married and Leah was doing cooking and cleaning duties. It is unclear.

But what is clear is that Joseph was a tattle tale on Zilpah, Bilhah and their sons. Remember who these ladies were, they were the maidservants of Leah and Rachel. So, in Joseph's mind, this part of his family was obviously below him and he felt like he should be in charge of them. Authority given too soon creates rebellion in others.

Verse 3 gives us a clue about this high and mighty attitude of Joseph. His father loved him the most out of all the sons (even Benjamin, who was the son of his right hand). He also hand-made him a tunic of many colours.

What was it about this tunic that was different from the other tunics that his brothers wore? My Bible states in the footnotes that the words 'many colours' might have been 'an inscription from another Semitic language, Akkadian which suggests an ornamented tunic as might be worn by royalty'.

This tunic represents more than just a covering to keep Joseph warm. It represents the calling that God had on his life. But just like Moses, Joseph acted on that calling out of God's will and it led to his downfall (albeit only for a short time).

In Exodus 2:11, Moses saw an Egyptian beating a Hebrew and so he killed the Egyptian. Moses' calling was to lead the Israelites out from under the Egyptian slavery but this was not the way or the time to do it.

Joseph's calling was in the palace but at 17 years old, this was not the place or the time allotted.

One person in the Bible who understood his calling and the timing of it was David. In 1 Samuel 16, David was anointed by Samuel the prophet to be king. But did David go out and pretend he was the king or even kill the king to speed up the calling? No, David just went back to being a shepherd in chapter 17. If you continue to read the story, David could have killed King Saul a number of times, but he would not lift his hand towards God's anointed leader. That was a man who knew the heart of God and the timing of God.

Often, in our own lives, we get this wrong. I have many times as I tried in my flesh to make myself known or seen through giftings that weren't mine. If I had known then what I know now, I would not have wasted my time but honed the skills in the areas that God called me to. Time and maturity in God is a great teacher.

Let's go back to our story. In verse 4, Joseph's brothers now hated him and wouldn't speak a kind word to him. This would have caused dissension and a break within the family. Mealtimes and other feast days would not have been a pleasant experience. Jealousy had overruled the love of the family and it was a hard taskmaster. Why? The ones who are jealous could become bitter and resentful and the other party could begin to allow pride to seep into their lives. The Bible tells us in Proverbs 16:18 that:

> *Pride goes before destruction,*
> *And a haughty spirit before a fall.*

There is nothing nice about bitter and resentful people and likewise a prideful person. This is a lose-lose situation and not a win-win for anybody.

But did this worry Joseph? No! In the very next verse, he decides to tell them a dream and did that go down well? NO! The brothers hated him even more.

There was no discernment in Joseph at all and definitely no compassion or empathy.

What made the brothers so riled up? Basically, he advised them that they would one day bow down to him and he would reign over them and have dominion over them.

The spoiling of Joseph by his father was becoming his downfall as an adult. Joseph knew he was loved more by his father and now he'd had a dream he would lord it over his brothers.

This wasn't looking good.

But then he dreamed another dream where even nature bowed down to him. For a God-fearing culture, this dream was too much for them. In verse 10, even Jacob is rebuking him, this son he loved so much.

Why? The interpretation of the dream, as told by Jacob, which was correct, was that Jacob represented the sun, Leah the moon and the eleven stars, his eleven brothers. So it was not nature bowing to him but his whole family.

The first dream encompassed only part of his family and the second dream included all of them.

Now not only did his brothers hate him, but they also envied him. They could see the calling on his life and they were not happy. This applies to us as well. We need to be happy when God calls someone else to a position we think is ours or should be ours. Only God knows what He has gifted us inside and that is not the same for everyone.

Remember the 10 talents story in Matthew 25:14. A man called his servants and delivered to them each some talents (or coins). To one of them he gave five, the next he gave two and to another one he gave one. God is not a fair God as not only has He created us uniquely, He has given us unique talents. The statement "God is not a fair God" may seem controversial to some. The definition of fair in the Oxford dictionary is treating people equally without favouritism or discrimination. If God was a fair God, He would have given all the servants the same amount of talents. But what good would that do if we could all sing but nobody could play an instrument or if we were all doctors and nobody was a chemist or if we were all cleaners and nobody could cook? It doesn't make much sense, does it? There are different talents as we are all different. Just remember that the next time you compare yourself to someone. You are not a clone but a unique son or daughter of God.

All the brothers had different callings from God and we can see that in the tribes of Israel later on in the Bible story. The brothers could have sought God and walked in their own callings but it was left to the generations to come to walk in the call of God. For example, Judah means 'praise' and he could have spent his days praising God and writing songs. Instead, he spent his days hating and despising his brother. Levi, likewise, was later called to be the priestly tribe of God.

But Levi could have walked in that calling and sought to get closer to God at that point but instead, he also spent his days hating and despising his brother.

In verse 12 of Genesis chapter 37, the brothers went to feed their father's flock in another place. It does not tell us which of his brothers were there so we will have to assume they all were, except for Benjamin, who may have been too young.

Then in verses 13 to 14, Jacob sent Joseph to his brothers to enquire about their safety and the safety of their flocks. This would have been a common occurrence as Joseph did not question his father regarding the journey.

He finally found them and in verse 18, as he was walking towards them, they conspired to kill him.

Reuben was the only one to try to talk them out of it. I am sure it was not out of a sense of obligation from the oldest brother, but he was already in trouble with his father and didn't want to add to that (see Genesis 35:22). He told them to put him in a pit and he would secretly rescue him later.

In verse 23, the brothers stripped him of his tunic. Does this sound familiar? It is the same as when Jesus lost his tunic on the way to the crucifixion. Joseph no longer had the tunic representing royalty and had, in the natural, lost the calling of God on his life. But even if outwardly our calling seems to be stripped from us, that can never happen unless we reject it.

It was Judah in verse 26 who decided that Joseph should be sold and not killed. Can you see the motivation of the brothers? Money was so important to them that they even sold their brother. They sold him for 20 shekels of silver (nearly the same amount Judas received for betraying Jesus).

Reuben was not involved in this as he obviously had gone away to do something for a while. So they dipped the tunic in goat's blood and took it to their father.

Jacob mourned for him and refused to be comforted. Were the dreams forgotten at this stage or did it seem impossible that they could now be fulfilled? In our lives, this can sometimes happen. Our dreams can be torn away from us and die for a while. Maybe it is because we left the town where God told us to plant a church. It could be that an illness has stopped you from writing or playing an instrument. Maybe you are housebound and feel that God has forgotten you and that calling on your life.

Dreams can seem to die for a while, but there is a trait that God needs to develop in each of us before our dreams can be fulfilled. What is it? It is character.

Let's think about Joseph for a minute. What kind of leader would he have been at this stage? He would probably have been an arrogant, prideful, non-godly leader who trampled on others so his will could be done.

God wants instead a kind, humble leader who has a heart for others, a servant heart and one that relies completely on God for everything.

In the next chapter, we will see what God does with Joseph who was not yet equipped to be a leader and had a lot of baggage to deal with.

Let's pray:

> *Father, we know that we also have a lot of baggage that we need to bring to you. At times, we are prideful, deceptive and flaunt the calling you gave us. Help us to trust completely in you and allow those character flaws to not take us out of our future but to drive us to it. In Jesus' name, amen.*

CHAPTER 3

# JOSEPH'S EARLY LIFE IN EGYPT

We left the last chapter with Joseph being sold to the Midianite traders. He is on his way, not to a life of royalty, not to a life of sonship, but to a life of being a servant. Servants were the lowest class in the household. They were to work hard and not be rewarded much. They were to endure whatever treatment the master meted out. It was not an ideal existence for anyone.

But through it all, God had a plan. If you feel like your life is at the bottom of the pit and there is nowhere further to fall, it's time to trust God for His plan. The life we find ourselves in today may not be the life planned for us by God. However, it may be a stepping stone in the tapestry that God is weaving.

Corrie ten Boom shared the tapestry story and it is where I first read it. If you look at one side of the tapestry, all you see are threads that don't seem to have a pattern, they are ratty and mostly tangled with other threads. Once you turn that tapestry over, a beautiful picture emerges. That side is what God sees—the beautiful picture of our life that He has planned for us. Most times all we see are the ratty and tangled threads that are every which way.

This is how Joseph must have looked at his life at this stage. The dreams he had were in the distance and didn't even seem they would be fulfilled. His brothers hated him and had plotted his downfall, so how would they ever bow down to him? But if God has given you a dream, you need to hang onto it and remind yourself of it, even when your life looks ratty and tatty.

We pick our story up in Genesis 37:36. It is just one verse, but it speaks multitudes. The Midianites sold Joseph in Egypt to Potiphar, an officer of Pharaoh and captain of the guard. Joseph stood in a line possibly with other people who were going to be sold. He was sold as a commodity, not as a man. Potiphar would have bid for him and money would have changed hands. It was literally a human auction. This would have been so degrading for Joseph and would have furthered his feelings of rejection and shame left over from his childhood.

Oftentimes, those things that affect us as children come back to haunt us as adults. This is not to break us but so we can deal with them. We will talk about some of these in the next few chapters.

God doesn't allow anything to touch our lives that will break us. It may feel like that at times, but it is so they come to the front and are dealt with, with God's help. God is far more interested in our character and making us more like Jesus than He is in our calling.

If we don't deal with our character flaws, then our calling may be delayed until they have been dealt with. If not, our character flaws will hurt others and that is not a good situation. Does this mean that God won't use us until we are perfect? Definitely not! But we won't be successful in our calling until we submit to God in everything, even our character flaws.

I'm going to touch on something here in relation to Joseph's brother, Judah. In Genesis 37:26, he was the one who instigated the selling of Joseph to the Midianite traders. He literally sold his brother. God did not take this well as Judah sinned against his brother. What were the consequences? We see them in Genesis 38. Judah left his brothers. This is what happened to Cain after he killed Abel. In Genesis 4:16, Cain went out from the presence of God. This is a dangerous place to be. No matter what happens in your life, keep living in the presence of God.

Judah leaving his brothers caused another family rift. Judah was not only leaving his family but was leaving the calling God had placed on his life. Judah married a woman and had three sons. His first son married a woman called Tamar. This was not a small amount of time but possibly close to the time that Joseph spent in Potiphar's house and then in prison.

In time, Judah's wife and first son died. Tamar was then married off to the second son and he also died. She then had to wait for the youngest son to grow up. When he did, he was not given in marriage to Tamar, so she crafted a plan to sleep with Judah. Out of that plan, she had twin sons. It was possibly after this time that Judah rejoined his family. His youngest son was not heard from again but Judah's line came through Tamar's two sons. What a mess!

Getting back to Joseph in Genesis 39, he had been purchased by Potiphar as a slave and was working in his house. Verse 2 is surprising given who Joseph was before he was sold as a slave. It states:

> *The Lord was with Joseph and he was a successful man;*
> *and he was in the house of his master the Egyptian.*

What? How could the Lord be with Joseph? As far as we could tell from the prior stories, Joseph didn't even have a relationship with God. It's in times of adversity that our relationship with God shines through the most. Why is that? Mainly because we have nowhere else to turn and no one else to trust.

Even though Joseph had been sold into slavery, God was with him. This should give us hope when we find ourselves in such a position. God is with us no matter what. The Bible does not tell us that Joseph walked out of the presence of God like Judah did. God was still with him. It is only when we walk out of the presence of God in our lives that God is not close to us. It's in these times that we open the door to

Satan and his schemes in our lives. Joseph didn't open that door, not even once.

The second thing that is astounding in verse 2 is that it states that Joseph was a successful man. How can you be successful in the position of a slave? What does successful even mean?

In the *Oxford Dictionary*, 'successful' means:

1. The fact that you have achieved something that you want and have been trying to do or get, the fact of becoming rich or famous or of getting a high social position
2. A person or thing that has achieved a good result and has been successful.

If we look at both of these definitions, neither one of them looks like the situation that Joseph found himself in. So obviously, God's idea of successful is far different from ours.

The Hebrew word for 'successful' is that God is the One who is causing the prospering or success to take place. The word literally means cutting a path through the forest and clearing it of shrubs and bushes and trees to make a clear path.

'Successful' is God making a way through for us when all we see is a forest or a dead end. For the Christian, success is always contingent on God being with us through everything.

The next part of this verse states that Joseph was in the house. He was not a slave of the land but of the house. The

*Jamieson-Fausset-Brown Bible Commentary* at www.biblehub.com on Genesis 39:2 provides us with some information regarding the house and the field slaves. The slaves who had been war captives were generally sent to labour in the field and subjected to hard treatment under the 'stick' of the taskmasters. However, those who were bought with money were generally employed in domestic services, were kindly treated and enjoyed more liberty.

Interestingly, Joseph never sought to escape from this place but put his trust in God. When had this trust in God begun? Joseph had heard the stories of creation, the fall, the flood and how God prospered his grandfather in a time of famine.

Stories don't make an impact on our lives until our lives line up with the stories. It's only in times of hardship that stories of people going through hardship really impact our lives. It was only on the journey from Dothan to Egypt that Joseph probably really cried out to God, maybe for the first time. He realised that only the hope of God and his trust in God could help him through whatever circumstances he found himself in Egypt. He probably knew that he was about to be sold but to whom and what would he be doing? When hard times come, it's easy to trust God as He is all there is to hold onto and to anchor ourselves to.

Verse 3 of Genesis 39 tells us that Potiphar saw that God was with Joseph and that it was God who made all prosper under Joseph's hand.

This is interesting to me. What was it about Joseph's words, character and attitude that told Potiphar that God was with him? How can we display this same behaviour today so that others may see Jesus? How did Potiphar even know there was a God?

I'm reminded of the story of Daniel. He also was taken captive from his home in Israel to Babylon in Daniel 1. It states in verse 17 of that chapter that God gave them (Daniel and his friends) knowledge and skill in all literature and wisdom and Daniel had understanding in all visions and dreams. Further, in verse 19, the king interviewed them and none was found like Daniel and his friends. In verse 20, it states that they were ten times better than all the magicians and astrologers in the king's realm.

Could it have been the same for Joseph? Did God somehow touch his life on the journey from Dothan to Egypt and give him the things he needed to be successful in the next position? He didn't give him money, but knowledge, wisdom and the ability to learn the language and customs of the Egyptians. Maybe it was Joseph's willingness to learn these things that made him different from the other slaves.

But I think it was also his attitude and his work ethic. From a young boy, he would have worked hard shepherding the sheep and doing other chores. The brothers may even have made him do more because he was one of the youngest. Whatever happened in his childhood had an impact on his adulthood in a good way.

Let's think about his character traits. Could he still be prideful now that he was a slave? Could he still have received favourable treatment now that he was a slave? Could he have acted as the favourite son if he now was a slave? The answer to all those questions is no. There would have been a big attitude adjustment on the journey from Dothan to Egypt.

Joseph's purpose in life would have also changed. He was no longer one of the brothers and a favoured one at that, carrying on his father's legacy. He was a slave whose purpose was to do good and keep himself alive.

Circumstances can change our perspectives on life and ourselves. I have seen it happen. In my own life, there was no room for selfishness once I became a mum and more so when I became a single mum. There is no room for pride in a single mum's life.

There are countless stories in the Bible where people changed for the better because their circumstances changed. For example:

1. Ruth—a foreigner who married an Israelite and whose family is in the lineage of Jesus
2. The apostle Paul—formerly called Saul, who persecuted and imprisoned Christians.
3. Peter—an unsaved fisherman who became the pillar of the Jewish church and who believed in Jesus.
4. David—a lone shepherd boy who became king.

5. Moses—an Israelite brought up in Pharaoh's palace who ended up in a wilderness before God called him to deliver his people out of Egypt.

All these people would have had character changes before they could fulfil the specific call of God in their lives.

Verse 4 states that Joseph found favour in Potiphar's sight and Joseph served him. Then he was promoted to overseer, and all was put under his authority. This is incredible. Potiphar was the captain of a guard and Joseph was second in charge to him in his household. What a step up! Joseph must have thought he had it made. But Potiphar's house was not Joseph's ultimate calling. It was a steppingstone to learn the language, culture and ways of the Egyptians.

So what was the result of Joseph's appointment? We find that in verse 5. God blessed the Egyptian's house and not only the people but everything that happened within the house and the field. Potiphar became blessed not because of his position but because of God's presence and influence on Joseph.

This is similar to what happened in 2 Samuel 6 in the story of when King David first attempted to bring the Ark of God to Jerusalem. A man was killed in this attempt as David tried to transport the ark the same way it came back to Israel from the Philistines' country a little while before. The ark was not meant to be transported by cart but to be carried on the shoulders of the Levites. The presence of God is not to be carried around on a cart but on His people.

Because of the tragedy that happened, David was afraid of God and didn't want the ark coming to Jerusalem so he put it inside the house of Obed-Edom, where it stayed for three months. What happened while the ark was there? In verse 11 of 2 Samuel 6, it tells us that God blessed Obed-Edom and all his household.

It was nothing that Obed-Edom did but was because of the Ark of God that the house was blessed. If we do the same and walk in the promises and statutes of God and in the presence of God, then we likewise will be blessed. It's not because of what we do, but because of God's presence. The absence of God's presence equals no blessing from God.

In verse 12, word gets back to King David that Obed-Edom's household and all that belongs to him are blessed by God. It wasn't only the people who were blessed, but everything that occurred within that house e.g. finances, bumper crops, nothing breaking down, animals being blessed, happiness in the house with no strife, etc.

King David couldn't miss out on this blessing, so he sought God and took the ark out of Obed-Edom's house the correct way and brought it to Jerusalem, where it belonged, in the temple of God.

This is exactly what happened in Potiphar's house when God was with Joseph as he worked in his house.

As stated before, Potiphar's house was not Joseph's final destination for his calling. As such, God had to orchestrate events in his life that would put him in the right position for his calling. God does that with us too. He can put us in painful circumstances, not to break us, but to allow us to move into our final calling.

Sometimes those circumstances entail a move to another country, it can be a move to another church, it can be the loss of a job that gives us a time of preparation, it can be a breakdown within a family that causes us to learn to trust God more or it could be any number of other things. God deals with each of us uniquely and He alone knows what we need and where we need to be to be in the position He needs us to be.

Joseph was not immune to this painful circumstance that was about to take place. I am glad this circumstance didn't happen to me but through everything, God is still with us unless we reject Him. The scripture in Romans 8:28 says that 'And we know that in all things God works for the good of those who love him, who have been called according to his purpose.' This applied to Joseph's circumstances, which we are going to explore next.

Note the words 'who have been called according to his purpose'. This means that God is working with us and positioning us in those places that He has called us to in His purpose and not ours. Our calling is generally never what we would pick for ourselves.

In verse 6 of Genesis 39, it tells us the appearance of Joseph. This is very rare in the Bible. This is so we don't compare our appearances with those in the Bible and decide it was their appearance that caused God to love them, for example.

But this time, the appearance is mentioned as it was the thing that led to Joseph's downfall within this household. I believe it was put in there as an example to us that it's not usually the fault of things in our control that cause our situation to change for the worse, but sometimes it's things outside our control. In Joseph's case, it was that he 'was handsome in form and appearance'. Not a lot he could have done about that.

It wasn't just anybody who noticed his appearance, but his master's wife. It was the top lady of the house. Be careful when top people notice you. It could be a trap or a test! She cast longing looks at Joseph (verse 7). She didn't only look at him once and then dismiss him, she looked at him for a little while until lust took over and she asked Joseph to lie with her. We need to be careful what we look at. The first glance is usually not our downfall but as we keep looking, it can be.

For example, we walk past the bakery on our way to do our shopping. If we glance in the bakery, we might see our favourite—apple pie. As we do our shopping, we might continually think about that apple pie. You know what happens next, right? You have to walk back past that bakery to get to your car and what screams at you 'buy me', but that apple pie. Do you resist temptation or not? That is the question. This seems a silly example, but it's what happens with other things in our lives too if we glance and then keep on thinking about it.

Adam and Eve had one tree that was forbidden, and they fell. Why? Because the temptation to know everything was irresistible. If they had resisted, the world today would be so totally different.

In verse 8, Joseph said no, he would not lie with her. For what reason, other than she is another man's wife? It was because of responsibility. Joseph was responsible for everything in the house except her. She was forbidden. But in verse 9, we see the real reason—Joseph says, 'How can I sin against God?' His real reason was his fear of God. The consequences before God of that sin would have been far greater than the consequences bestowed on him by the husband.

Joseph by now had a fear of God around his life. He could see that it was God who prospered him and not himself.

Who knows temptation doesn't go away on the first no? We have to be resolute in our no, especially when we fear God. We can't fall into the enemy's trap. In verse 10, we read that the wife kept badgering him day by day, but Joseph did not heed her (he took no notice of her). The fear of God kept him from sinning.

If words don't work in temptation, what could? Aloneness! If Satan can't tempt you to do the thing with words, he will wait until you are alone somewhere and continue the badgering. This is the time you need support so you're not pulled away. Aloneness never solves anybody's issues, but community always does. Exposure of sin always brings it to light but hiding sin is only done in darkness. Most thieves only steal at night when they think nobody can see them. Worse still is when we think God can't see us.

In verse 11, she finally got Joseph alone (no other men were in the house with him). Then she caught him by the garment and again said, 'Lie with me.' The temptation was still the same, but the execution wasn't. Satan will try many ways of execution to make you sin but you must be strong in God.

In verse 12, it tells us that Joseph fled and ran outside. I am not sure where he fled to but he was still a slave so we know he would have stayed on the property. When temptation gets that bad, run from it (whatever that looks like in your circumstances). For example, close social media, close the library app, don't answer the phone call from your ex-boyfriend/girlfriend, unfollow people on Facebook, plan your journey around those tempting shops, etc. Just flee!

This woman was sneaky. In verse 14, she called the men of the house and then lied to them. Joseph might have been put in charge of the household, but he was still a foreigner. He was someone the wife didn't really like or maybe she had a favourite man she was hoping would be promoted instead. We won't really ever know why she hated Joseph. The moral of the story—love can sometimes be disguised as hate.

The woman's motive was not because she loved Joseph but because she hated him. We need to test the motives of people and not fall into the trap of deception and lies. The woman's first words were deceiving, not loving.

She then told her husband when he came home and he found Joseph and put him in prison. It was not any prison but the king's prison (verse 20). This was where the king's prisoners were kept. Where better to be held than the king's prison where the stories and goings on of the palace would have been talked about? This was going to hold Joseph later on when he stood before the king. But he didn't know that.

Verse 21 is probably one of the most comforting scriptures we will read in the Bible. Joseph had just been put in prison and the start of that verse reads:

> *But the Lord was with Joseph and showed him mercy, and He gave Him favour.*

What? In a prison cell? Yes, God can show us favour anywhere as long as we are in His will and His plan for our lives.

The keeper of the prison put the whole prison in his hands. Once again, Joseph was in a leadership position but this time instead of leading an official's house, he was leading the prisoners. Joseph was learning to lead wherever he was placed. That is a lesson to us. Your calling will shine through wherever God has placed you. It's up to us, in each circumstance, good or bad, to be willing to operate in it.

The last verse of the chapter states that whatever Joseph did, the Lord made it prosper. This should be our heart's cry. 'Lord, whatever I do for you, make it prosper.'

We are going to pause Joseph's story here so we can consider the prisons some of us have been placed in or place ourselves in before we talk about how to be set free from them.

Let's pray:

*Father, I thank you that Joseph's story has shown us so much already of Your will and Your ways and how it pertains to our lives. We thank you for his example and that his story shows that You are with us always, in the good times and the bad. Thank you. In Jesus' name, amen.*

CHAPTER 4

# PRISON OF INSECURITY

The prison of insecurity is one where we can find ourselves living for many years, if we don't recognise it and deal with it.

In the *Oxford Dictionary*, 'insecurity' means uncertainty or anxiety about oneself; or lack of confidence. In the *Oxford Dictionary*, 'confidence' means the feeling or belief that one can have faith in or rely on someone or something.

If we look at these two definitions together, insecurity means a lack of faith or relying on ourselves. In other words, we don't trust ourselves to do something right, say something right or act the right way.

Joseph didn't seem to have a problem with insecurity once he grew up, but his brothers did. Joseph knew who he was and what his calling was but his brothers didn't. The result was that Joseph fulfilled his calling but his brothers only lived a mediocre life (nothing noteworthy happened). If we want to live an abundant life like Jesus has for us in John 10:10 and make a difference in the world we live in, we must overcome our prison of insecurity.

How do we do this? Is it by relying on ourselves more or is it relying on our creator? Our insecurities will only be broken once we realise that God is passionately in love with us, that His plans and purposes for our life are good and that we can totally trust and rely on and have faith in Him because He only delivers good.

This sounds like a big ask, doesn't it? But it is possible. How do I know? Because I have lived in the prison of insecurity and have been set free from it. Sometimes, if I am not careful, I can fall back into the trap but temptation will always come. If it comes, we can always resist it.

My story starts at birth when I was adopted into another family. This family was great but as I grew up, I realised that more and more I was not like them. I didn't think like the rest of the family, I didn't act like the rest of the family, I had different tastes and interests and it made me feel very insecure. As a child, insecurity can come when we don't fit into the mould around us. I definitely didn't fit in. My family loved me a lot but it was probably like living with a stranger, even though I had been there since birth.

Another thing that contributed to my insecurity, or was as a result of my insecurity, was my incredible shyness. Shyness can stem from insecurity; a shy child will not be the centre of attention, will be well-behaved because they don't want to say or do anything wrong and will often be overlooked.

The definition from *The Light Program*[2] states that being secure as a person is related to standards that are set by the people we have close contact with, such as our family, friends and work colleagues, and expectations that are set by society that may be real or imagined. Insecurities develop when we compare ourselves to others and feel less than others. They occur when we experience a consequence for being different from others in a perceived negative way or when we feel we do not measure up to where we 'should' be.

We can see from this definition that insecurities can develop through comparison. This is seen clearly in the life of Rachel, Joseph's mother. Her insecurities caused jealousy between her and her sister Leah which was possibly never resolved.

Once Rachel died, Joseph may have, in his younger years (before the dreams), suffered the same insecurities as his mother. Maybe that's why Jacob gave him his multi-coloured coat, so he would feel worthy as his son.

There are a lot of emotional stories in the life of Joseph that are not clear on the surface but become clear as we delve into the history of the family and look at Joseph's reactions to his own circumstances.

---

2 https://thelightprogram.pyramidhealthcarepa.com/insecurities-impact-mental-health/

Another person in the Bible who suffered from insecurities was King Saul. His kingly story started when Israel demanded a king so they could be like all the nations around them (1 Samuel 8). God gave in to their demands (even though it was not His best; God does this with us too) and told Samuel the prophet to go to a certain city and God would send him a man to anoint the first king of Israel (1 Samuel 9:16).

Saul and his servant were going to this city too because they wanted to find out what happened to the donkeys they were looking for and went searching for the prophet so he could advise them (1 Samuel 9:6–10). God orchestrated this meeting as neither Samuel nor Saul lived in this town.

In 1 Samuel 10:1, Samuel anoints Saul as commander or king over the Israelites. What does Saul then do? He just goes home.

Then in 1 Samuel 10:17, Samuel calls all the people together at Mizpah to show them their new king. Samuel announces him but he is nowhere to be found. In verse 22, God told them that he was hiding in the equipment, so they found him and brought him forward.

Talk about insecurity! Saul was so insecure he hid from his calling. Have you ever found yourself doing that? God has called you to do something but your insecurities have you hiding instead of obeying. I have many times and my insecurity says it's too hard, nobody likes me, I can't talk to people, I'm an introvert, I'm not good at that and my favourite thing (writing) is my weakest skill.

Insecurity happens to us all. Insecurity is really all about me and dissipates when I remember it's all about God. If God has called me, He will equip me.

I remember a situation at work many years ago. I received a promotion and was successful ahead of around 40 people who were considered for the position. I knew I could not do this job in my own strength, so I prayed, 'God, You gave me this job, You equip me for it.' He did. When we give our insecurities over to God, He steps in. I love that verse in 2 Corinthians 12:9–10, which states:

> *And He said to me, "My grace is sufficient for you, for My strength is made perfect in weakness." Therefore, most gladly I will rather boast in my infirmities, that the power of Christ may rest upon me. Therefore, I take pleasure in infirmities, in reproaches, in needs, in persecutions, in distresses, for Christ's sake. For when I am weak, then I am strong.*

When I am weak in my insecurity, God's grace enables me to be strong because I'm resting in His strength and not my own.

It's only a few short chapters further along but probably a number of years later when Saul's insecurity costs him his calling.

Samuel told Saul to go and fight against Amalek and destroy everything—the livestock and the people and the town. This was a punishment from God for their wrongdoing against Israel as they had ambushed them in the wilderness many years before. God never forgets an injustice done to His people.

Saul and the army went out, but they didn't obey God fully. Who knows that that is dangerous? They spared the king and the best of the livestock. The king was a trophy in the palace and the livestock was to sacrifice to God. Look at the motives—they seemed to be right but were so wrong. God told them to destroy everything, not most of it.

When Samuel confronted Saul over his disobedience, Saul had all the excuses. In verse 24 of 1 Samuel 15, we read:

> *Then Saul said to Samuel, "I have sinned, for
> I have transgressed the commandment of the
> Lord and your words, because I feared the people
> and obeyed their voice."*

If we are not secure in our calling and the things that God has told us to do, insecurities will rule and result in our downfall. Insecurities lead to fear of people. This can take many forms, e.g. shyness, not speaking up for what is right, not obeying God, looking to others for approval instead of God, wanting to be in the popular group instead of being friends with those God puts in your path, being jealous of other people and their calling, etc.

We need to deal with our insecurities through prayer and counselling, if required.

Let's look at a king who knew he had insecurities but went to God instead. This is not King David, although he dealt with his well, but his son, King Solomon. In 1 Kings 3, the chapter heading is 'Solomon Requests Wisdom'. Wisdom will always help us through our insecurities and in Proverbs 4:7, it states:

*Wisdom is the principal thing: Therefore, get wisdom.*
*And in all your getting, get understanding.*

Wisdom is the main thing that will assist us in everything in our Christian walk. But it is not our wisdom that is the main thing but God's wisdom. If we don't have God's wisdom, then each day we need to ask for it, as James 1:5 states.

In verse 5 of 1 Kings 3, it states that the Lord appeared to Solomon in a dream by night and asked him a question—what shall I give you? If God asked that question of you, what would you say? Most of us would say health, wealth, etc., something that would generally affect only ourselves and maybe our families. Solomon's insecurities drove him to ask for wisdom but he doesn't start his discourse off like that with God. Instead, he lists all his insecurities:

- Verse 6—you were with my dad and showed him great kindness and that kindness has extended to me as his successor. Solomon knew he was only in the position because of the grace and kindness of God. David had many sons and God could have chosen any one of them, but He chose Solomon.

- Verse 7—the insecurities start to come out. Solomon told God he was only a little child who didn't know how to go out or come in. He was basically saying, 'God, I am so insecure. I feel like a little child who has lost his way and I need guidance. This calling is too big for me.'
- Verse 8—then Solomon considered the task and the multitude of people God had given him to rule over. Solomon is possibly looking at the people and saying, 'It's me against all of them. What do I know?' Not only was the calling too great but the task was too. Just to clarify, we might be called to be a pastor, but it could be to 50 people or 5000. The calling is the same, but the task is vastly different.
- Verse 9—this is where Solomon made his request known. Solomon wanted an understanding heart—one that understood what was going on and why. He wanted to be able to discern between good and evil because sometimes the situations we come across can look nearly the same. He wanted to be able to judge righteously and see through to what was really going on. These are good traits to have or ask for if you are a leader and you don't have them. Leaders need understanding. They need to be able to judge righteously, be able to discern what is really going on and have a heart for people.

Solomon's insecurities were dissolved once God granted his request and gave him wisdom. Solomon understood it was nothing he'd done, but what God had done.

When we give our insecurities to God, He exchanges them for strengths. He exchanges our shyness for boldness. He exchanges our fear of people for fear of God. He exchanges our perceived lack of skills for His calling on our lives. He exchanges our bonds for His anointing.

In my life, I have found that the insecurities I carry need to be worked on daily. A situation will always arise where my insecurities want to rule but I need to exchange them for God's wisdom daily. That's why it's imperative that we ask for God's wisdom on a daily basis.

Jesus didn't carry any insecurities whilst He walked on the earth. This was not because He is God but because He knew His purpose and every day He received His orders from God and carried them out. He didn't allow people to control His emotions.

John 7 tells the story of Jesus and the Feast of Tabernacles. This was a feast of seven days. In verse 3, his brothers urged him to go to Judea so Jesus could do miracles and works there for all to see. But in verse 8, Jesus tells them to go to the feast and that He hasn't yet been released by God to go. Jesus was secure in what He was supposed to do each day and He didn't let anyone else persuade Him from the course.

Jesus eventually did go up secretly (verse 8). In verse 14, in the middle days of the feast, Jesus went to the temple and taught. The teaching He gave at this time shows us how secure He was in the calling and purpose of God in His life. It states, in verses 16 to 17 that:

> *"My doctrine is not Mine, but His who sent me. If anyone wills to do His will, he shall know concerning the doctrine, whether it is from God or whether I speak on My own authority."*

Then in verse 28, Jesus speaks and says:

> *"You both know Me, and you know where I am from; and I have not come of Myself, but He who sent Me is true, whom you do not know. But I know Him, for I am from Him, and He sent Me."*

Jesus knew where He came from and He knew what His purpose was, and as long as He stuck with that, insecurities were not going to get Him.

The purpose of Jesus is clearly outlined in Acts 10:38. It states:

> *... how God anointed Jesus of Nazareth with the Holy Spirit and with power, who went about doing good and healing all who were oppressed by the devil, for God was with Him.*

Let's break this verse down in relation to security. We can be secure by knowing these things:

1. God has anointed each one of us who has repented and is a Christ follower. In 2 Corinthians 1:21–22, it states:

    *Now He who establishes us with you in Christ and has anointed us is God, who also has sealed us and given us the Spirit in our hearts as a guarantee.*

    In the Bible, 'anointed' means consecrated or made sacred, dedicated to God.[3]

    Just like Jesus needed the anointing of God, so do we. The anointing sets our identity. We are no longer our own—we were brought with a price, that of Jesus dying on the cross to redeem us of our sins, etc. When Jesus did that, He opened the way for us to have a relationship with God and in choosing God, He has anointed us.

2. There were two anointings that Jesus needed—the Holy Spirit and power. The Holy Spirit was given to the disciples on the day of Pentecost. The Holy Spirit

---

[3] www.dictionary.com

alighted on Jesus when He was baptized by water. The Holy Spirit is our comforter, guide and confidante. He is necessary in our lives if we want to walk like Jesus did.

The second one is power. Jesus received the power when He came out of the wilderness after being tempted for 40 days. In Luke 4:14, it states:

> *Then Jesus returned in the power of the Spirit to Galilee and news of Him went out through all the surrounding region.*

Jesus came out of the wilderness in power and we will do the same. A wilderness experience is not meant to break us but to empower us to overcome the next challenge. It's a time when our walk with God deepens, our character is challenged and corrected, and our trust in God deepens. It's a place of necessity, not punishment. It's time to treat the wilderness as lessons to be learnt and not a punishment to be endured.

3. Jesus went about doing good. He knew what His purpose was and did it. For many of us, insecurities come when we don't know our purpose. We compare ourselves to others and come up short. The issue is that what others are doing is not what we are called to do.

My insecurities come when my value is being eroded. But this is also self and when we are totally following God's purpose for our lives, there's no time for self. Jesus didn't go about doing good for Himself. He didn't spend His time on leisure pursuits like going fishing or tying knots or whatever they did back then. He was not selfish but absorbed in others. Once we find out our calling and start operating in it to do good for others, there will be no room for insecurities.

4. Jesus healed all who were oppressed by the devil. When you are dealing with people who are being oppressed, there is no time for insecurities either. Why? Because we know God has anointed us and called us to do specific things. Even though we may feel inadequate, we remind ourselves often that if God has called us to do something, only He can empower us to do it. I can't do what God has called me to do in my own strength. It's not possible.

What does 'oppressed' mean? In the *Oxford Dictionary*, it means subject to harsh and authoritarian treatment. Where does this come from? In the Bible, it states from the devil. The devil is out to steal, kill and destroy (John 10:10). But Jesus' ministry was all about freeing people from that oppression. Ours should be too.

How? There are a number of ways:

- Listening to a person's story and providing them with answers from God
- Praying over someone who is sick so they get healing from God
- Speaking a kind word over someone who has had a bad week
- Buying a gift for someone, e.g. a coffee, to show you care and they are not on their own
- Taking them to church so they hear an uplifting word
- Praying that God will free those in addiction
- Speaking to kids in children's ministry and telling them that God is with them and He is their best friend
- Reminding the young people that God has a purpose for their lives and not to lose hope

There are countless ways we can minister to people who are oppressed.

5. The last part of that verse sums up why Jesus could do what He did and why we can do what God calls us to do. God is with us. In Hebrews, it tells us that God will never leave us or forsake us. This means that God is with us always and He will not leave even when we sin against Him. The relationship on our part will be

> broken but once we repent, it will be restored. That's how loving our God is.
>
> But what is really important in this part of the verse is that Jesus needed to know God was with Him too. Jesus prayed constantly to God, which means He spoke to His Father throughout the day. I am guilty of not doing this often. I don't know sometimes whether we think God doesn't care or think that He is responsible for the situations we find ourselves in, but I need to be reminded that God is with me and the only way that can happen is if I talk to Him daily.

Insecurities in our life will only arise when we don't have a purpose, aren't helping others, don't know who we are in God and don't remember that God is with us.

So other than Jesus, who else in the Bible dealt well with insecurities? The most obvious example to me is David.

Saul had already been anointed king by God (and subsequently rejected by God) when David was anointed. The anointing of the new king didn't happen through the family line and nor was it when Saul died. God wanted to raise up a young man who loved Him and showed signs of trusting Him so He could work with and develop Him into his role as king.

David was anointed king at a young age but not because of looks or rank in the family as we find out in 1 Samuel 16. David didn't even get to go to the feast with his dad and brothers as he had to mind the sheep. This was a young man who in his family's eyes was not worthy of being invited. Have you ever felt like that? I have many times. But in reading the story, David didn't even bring this up. Sometimes we need to let this seeming rejection pass us by as in God's timing, we can't be uninvited.

Let's look at the story in more detail. In verse 1, God sent Samuel to Jesse (David's father) as God had provided for Himself a king from one of his sons. Samuel had reservations—what if King Saul heard about him anointing another king? If he did, Samuel would be killed. But God said go and he went.

Samuel arrived in the village and invited Jesse and his sons to the sacrifice. Samuel meant all of Jesse's sons, but Jesse only brought the ones he considered worthy or of age.

Before they ate, Jesse's sons were paraded before Samuel from the oldest to the youngest. None of them were chosen. Finally, Samuel asked Jesse if he had another son; sure he had heard from God.

Jesse said yes but he was keeping the sheep. This son was more like a hired hand than a son because his father didn't even include him. Jesse called for David, and he came. David could have pouted and said he wasn't coming because he hadn't been invited in the first place, but he didn't feel insecure in the job he was doing for his father or of his place in the family. He came and Samuel anointed him.

Did David act high and mighty and advise his father he was not keeping the sheep anymore? No, David went right back to doing what he had always done.

How do we know this? In 1 Samuel 17, David's three older brothers went off to fight the Philistines. David was back at his father's house from the palace (1 Samuel 17:14) feeding the sheep. Jesse told David to take provisions to his brothers, which he did. But first, he left the sheep with a keeper. He arrived at the battle as Goliath was speaking his daily threats.

The army fled at these threats but did David flee too? No, because he knew Who His God was. David offered to go and fight the giant. The king thought that was foolish and so did the others because David was not a man of war but a youth. Did David let the insecurity of his age tell him what to do? No, he recounted the stories of how God had saved him from a lion and a bear and that God would be with him. There was not an insecurity to be found in David's life. Why? Because he knew Who His God was.

David brought down Goliath with a slingshot and one stone and then beheaded him. The Philistines were then defeated by the Israelite army.

The lesson here is that if God is with us, those things around our lives where we feel insecure should fade into oblivion when we remember Who our God is. God created us exactly as we are with talents, dreams and plans for our future. If we trust in and rely on God, our insecurities will go away.

Let's pray:

*Father, we thank you that You are always with us.*
*We pray about any insecurities we have around our*
*lives and we bring them to you and ask that You help us*
*deal with them and remind us of Whose we are.*
*We thank you, Father, that you created us and we know*
*that we are to work with you on anything that hinders*
*us in our walk with you. Please forgive us for doubting*
*your love and forgetting that you are with us.*
*In Jesus' name, amen.*

CHAPTER 5

# PRISON OF DOUBT

Doubt is one of those words that can apply to any area of our lives. In the *Oxford Dictionary*, 'doubt' means a feeling of uncertainty or lack of conviction. Uncertainty comes to us when we are not certain of a thing.

Some areas of doubt for us could be:

- We doubt that God will be there for us
- We doubt that God's plan will come to pass
- We doubt that God's word is true
- We are uncertain that what we believe is actually true
- We are uncertain that anything good will ever happen in our lives
- We are uncertain that God only has good plans for us and not evil

- We doubt that anybody will ever love us or be our friend
- We doubt we will ever get married and have children
- We doubt we will ever get the job we really want
- We doubt we will ever get out of debt

The danger of doubt is that we live in a constant negative mindset and start to see the world in shades of black and grey. Doubt prevents us from seeing God in all His fullness and majesty. Doubt dims our seeing, hearing and speaking.

Jesus spoke about doubt in relation to faith. Doubt is not the opposite of faith but doubt will lead to us being double-minded and therefore not receiving anything from God (James 1:6-8).

Joseph would have had many times of doubt, especially when he was down the pit, on his way to Egypt as a slave, in Potiphar's house and definitely whilst he was in jail.

While the Bible is unclear on how Joseph coped with doubt in these circumstances, we can assume that sometimes he let doubt creep in and get to him. What was it that Joseph probably doubted? It was the promise from God that one day his brothers would bow down to him and so would the sun, moon and stars. These promises would have seemed too far away down a pit, in a slave trader's caravan or a jail cell. But even when we doubt, the promises of God still come to pass if we only have a mustard seed (small amount) of faith.

Before we have a look at a couple of stories in the Bible and people who doubted and the consequences of that doubt or people who believed despite of doubt, let's look at a few stories where Jesus confronted doubt.

1. In a boat

    Let's read the story titled, 'Wind and Waves Obey Jesus' in Mark 4:35–41.

    In verse 35, Jesus and his disciples got into the boat and Jesus said, 'Let us cross over to the other side.' Then Jesus went to the stern and fell asleep.

    However, in verse 37, the Bible states that a great windstorm arose and the waves were beating at the boat and water was coming in. These seasoned fishermen were terrified. They forgot the word that Jesus had spoken earlier about crossing over to the other side. When we forget the Word of God, doubt will always creep in and then take up residence.

    They woke up Jesus and told him that the boat was going down. Jesus stood up and rebuked the wind and the waves and they ceased.

    But in verse 40, Jesus declares the words that are still true in our lives today. They are 'Why are you so fearful? How is it that you have no faith?'

When we doubt the Word of God, we don't only open ourselves up to doubt but also to fear. Fear, in turn, leads our faith walk into non-existence. We can doubt for a moment as a thought comes in, but it is when we stay in doubt that the door opens wider to let in more dangerous things.

Fear will come marching in anytime we let doubt linger as fear is the opposite of faith. Faith believes, whereas fear always doubts. For example, we believe for finances, and they don't arrive on our time schedule. We doubt the provision of God for our lives and then fear comes in and says we'll be evicted for not paying the rent. Fear always believes the worst.

2. Thomas

In John 20:19–23, after Jesus was resurrected, He appeared to His disciples. The disciples at that time were shut up in a room together for fear of the Jews. These men had seen what had happened to Jesus and thought that they were next.

The first thing Jesus said was, 'Peace be with you.' Jesus wanted to ensure that His peace was with them. He showed the disciples His hands and His side, which were nailed and pierced respectively in the crucifixion. They were so happy to see Jesus.

However, there was one disciple who wasn't with them at that time (for whatever reason) —Thomas.

Jesus left and Thomas came back, and the disciples told him they had seen Jesus. What was Thomas' reaction? It was doubt. In verse 25 of chapter 20, Thomas said:

> *"Unless I see in His hands the print of the nails, and put my finger into the print of the nails, and put my hand into His side, I will not believe."*

Thomas not only didn't believe the story, he wanted evidence. Not only that, he wanted to experience it with his senses.

This states to me that there are three stages of doubt.

1. The first is not believing someone's story or experience. The only reason we don't believe is that we don't trust the person telling the story.

    If it is a good friend telling us the story or even when we are reading the Word of God, we need to trust the good friend or the author of the Bible—God. In these situations, we need to ask ourselves why we don't trust.

2. The second is that we need evidence the story really happened. This means that not only do we not trust the person; we think they are lying to us and their story is false.

   But are the stories and experiences of the people in the Bible lies or are they truth? If they are truth, then we can trust. We must believe the story really happened.

3. The third is that we need to be involved in the story. We would need to physically be there, see video evidence or maybe a photo. This means that not only don't we trust the person; we think the story is false but we will only believe when we experience it.

   This stage of doubt is dangerous as it leads to deep distrust taking place in our hearts. We get to the place where we will only see the negative in everything and our trust of people and ultimately of God are damaged.

   This is a stronghold over our lives that will need to be prayed over and broken. It is a dangerous place to live.

As stated above, any of those stages can lead us into not trusting God's Word or even God. This means that we are not walking by faith but by sight. In Hebrews 11:6 it states that it is impossible to please God without faith. If we are walking like this, we are not pleasing God.

Did Jesus leave Thomas in his doubt? No, and He will not do that to us either. However, it took eight days for Jesus to come and deal with the doubt in Thomas. Doubt is not an easy fix but can take time to remedy. It will take a deliberate action on our part to just believe.

In John 20:27, Jesus speaks to Thomas and says:

> *"Reach your finger here, and look at My hands; and reach your hand here, and put it into My side. Do not be unbelieving, but believing."*

Even though Jesus met Thomas where He was, Jesus rebuked him for his unbelief. But Jesus didn't leave it there with the rest of the disciples either. He stated in verse 29, "Because you have seen Me, you have believed. Blessed are those who have not seen and yet have believed."

There was a warning to the rest of the disciples, including Thomas, and to all who would read or hear the Bible in that statement. Blessing will only come when we don't doubt but believe. Believe what? Believe in not only Who Jesus is but also what Jesus did.

Verse 30–31 really sums this up and states:

> *And truly Jesus did many other signs in the presence of His disciples, which are not written in this book; but these are written that you may believe that Jesus is the Christ, the Son of God, and that believing you may have life in His Name.*

Those verses sum up the blessing of God from believing and that is eternal life with Jesus and God both here on earth and in heaven later. Such an amazing blessing!

Let's have a look at a couple of other stories in the Bible where people doubted and were rebuked and had cause to doubt but didn't.

1. Adam and Eve—doubted

    Most of us know the story of Adam and Eve in the Garden of Eden and that's what we are going to touch on here.

    In Genesis 2:15–17, God gave Adam clear instructions regarding his food supply. He could eat of every tree in the garden except for one. Can you imagine what that would have been like? There would have been a multitude of fruit trees and nut trees that he could have partaken of. There were probably trees there of things we have never heard of. But there was only one tree he couldn't eat from.

    When Eve was created, we assume Adam told her the same story exactly how God had said it.

    But there came a day, when that 'one' tree was too powerful to resist. The serpent came to tempt Eve not by stealth but by using doubt. Doubt in the words that God had spoken regarding that one tree.

This happens to us too. Don't go one kilometre or mile over the speed limit. Don't tell even one white lie. Don't steal even one thing. Don't say one bad word to someone else etc. We still sin over that 'one' thing.

The serpent starts the conversation with 'Has God indeed said ...?' This should have rung alarm bells. The serpent is trying to get her to doubt. Once Eve doubted the word from God, she started to doubt the consequences of disobedience. We do the same.

We think we won't get caught speeding, telling lies, speaking nastily, etc., but we do and the consequences of disobedience catch up with us.

Eve ate the fruit and then Adam did likewise, but God was not happy. Not only did they disobey and eat and lose their eternal life in the Garden of Eden, but other things crept into their lives like shame, insecurity and worthlessness.

Doubt will take us further than we want to go down the disobedience path.

2. Abraham—doubted

    Abraham's story starts at the end of Genesis 11 and continues for a number of chapters.

    Abraham received lots of promises from God but the one that had him doubting was regarding his descendants. When we read the story of Abraham,

God did three different things in Abraham's life to keep his faith strong in this area, but he still fell. Those three things were:

1. God took Abram outside and showed him the stars and told him to count them if he was able to. Obviously, it's too hard to count every star as there are multitudes of them. Then God said in Genesis 15:5, 'So shall your descendants be.'

    In verse 6, it states:

    > *And he believed in the Lord, and He accounted it to him for righteousness.*

    Abraham believed God but would seeing be enough to allay his doubts?

2. God cut a covenant with Abram in Genesis 15:9–21. A covenant cut between two people or tribes, or God and us is binding. It can never be broken. A covenant is when a person/tribe/God joins with another person or tribe generally because they each have something the other one wants or desires. There is always blood shed in a covenant to seal the deal. This is what Jesus did for us on the cross. The only way we could be reconciled to God was through Jesus shedding His blood for us

on the cross. God wanted a reconciled family and we needed a Saviour.

God cut a covenant with Abram. God wanted Abram to believe in Him for descendants, who would become the Israelites, the children of God and Abram wanted descendants.

In verse 18, again God reiterated that Abram would have descendants.

Before we go onto the third way, in Genesis 16, Abram doubted and fell. He had relations with Hagar, which resulted in a son, Ishmael. Abram took matters into his own hands. This was not God's promise but man's choice. When we doubt, we can handle matters our way, which never works out and always causes pain and hardship.

3. In Genesis 17, God did the last thing that would cause Abram to believe—He changed his name from Abram to Abraham. This meant that every time someone spoke his name or he did, he would hear 'father of many nations'. A little while later, Isaac was born and the promise was fulfilled.

The remedy for us doubting is to always speak the promise from God. Too often, we expect instant miracles instead of the building of our character and trust in God as our faith is developed.

Who trusted God when they could have doubted?

1. Noah was instructed to build an ark as God was going to send rain. He did it even though it had never rained on Earth and what was rain anyway? The ground at that time was watered from underneath (Genesis 2:5–6).
2. Esther believed God when the Israelites were going to be annihilated by Haman and put her life on the line to go before the king, even though she risked her life in doing so.
3. Hezekiah sent singers out in front of the army as he had been instructed to fight the battle, instead of the army going first.

All the above things sound strange, but it was in their obedience to God that caused their doubt to turn to faith and courage.

God wants to do the same for you and me. He wants to turn our doubts about who we are and what He wants us to do into faith and courage. Courage is when we do what God asks even though we are afraid. Faith keeps our eyes on God as we journey through life.

The main thing that doubt does in our lives and keeps us securely locked in the prison is in relation to fulfilling the plans, purpose and calling of God on our lives.

Matthew 28:18–20 states:

> *And Jesus came and spoke to them, saying, "All authority has been given to Me in heaven and on earth. Go, therefore and make disciples of all the nations, baptising them in the name of the Father and of the Son and of the Holy Spirit, teaching them to observe all things that I have commanded you; and lo, I am with you always, even to the end of the age."*

There is no room in this verse for the prison of doubt to come in and tell us that we don't have what it takes to do the will of God for our lives. Jesus said 'go' and that is what He means. There is no room for excuses in the word 'go'.

If we come back to the meaning of 'doubt' in the *Oxford Dictionary*, it means to feel uncertain about or to feel fear or be afraid. Not only does doubt force us to question ourselves, but it also forces us to question God. Doubt will never let us walk further in life than we currently are and in fact, if we are stagnant for too long, we will drift backwards.

It's like we're on a body board. We jump onto it and start paddling out to where the big waves are. We're really excited to finally be back on the body board after a long year at work. But all of a sudden, we look up and the waves seem bigger than we remember. We have gone out too far and now cannot touch the bottom with our feet. Doubts start to come into our minds. Do I have the skills for this? Do I still remember how to body board? What happens if a shark comes by? Maybe I just won't make it to shore. What happens if I lose my body board even though it's tied to me?

Excitement has given way to doubt and if we don't arrest it in our minds, fear will eventually come in and paralyse us. What was meant to be an enjoyable day at the beach could quickly turn into a panic attack.

This is how we are with God. We know the verse in Jeremiah 29:11 about the good plans and the good future that God has for our lives. We have heard God clearly speak to us about the next step in our lives and are very excited. But then doubts start coming in. They take the form of:

1. I don't have the skills.
2. This skill is my worst one. Others are better than me.
3. I don't have the finances to go to Bible College or back to university or college.
4. I don't have time to do this.
5. What if I mess this opportunity up?
6. What if people look at me and judge that I am not capable?
7. What if I look at someone else and think God has chosen the wrong person?

This was my life from 2015 to 2022 when I released my first book. God had given me the title of the book and the chapters. But then doubts started to come in. Every time I felt prompted to write, I would write a bit and then stop. There was no consistency because self-doubt would arise. People told me I hadn't heard from God or maybe this was just something that God had given me for myself.

I knew I didn't have the skills as writing is my weakest skill in my daily work life. Besides all that, I had no idea how to get an editor, how I was going to sell it and how to even put a book together.

What kept me going through all that time was knowing I had a word from God. I had no support coming from anywhere other than God.

How did I finish that book and self-publish it? God yelled at me to finish it at the start of 2022. You do not want to be yelled at by God. His voice overcame the doubts in my head and I finished and self-published that book in September 2022. How did I do it? By trusting in God and following His leading and divine providence for me every step of the way. When you know without a doubt that God is with you and it's His plan for your life, any doubts you have will be whittled away to nothing.

Do I still doubt? Yes, but I have learned in those times to listen to the still, small voice of God. When doubts are screaming at you, take yourself into your quiet place (wherever that may be) and listen to the voice of God. God is speaking to us all the time but we need to train ourselves to hear His voice. It's similar to tuning the radio to the correct radio station we want to listen to. Radio stations speak into our lives. But we want to tune our spirit into the station where God speaks.

If you are having issues, just be quiet for a few minutes and say to God, 'Do You love me?' He will always answer yes and now you have heard the voice of God you can practice daily being attuned to it.

The prison of doubt can only come down as we know that we are God's children and He is our loving heavenly Father. It will come down when we learn to hear the voice of God and obey His voice regardless of whether we think what God is telling us is silly or not.

The prison will come down when we realise that God doesn't need us to have the talents and resources for the things He has called us to do. He only requires our obedience and our willingness to say yes.

Will you allow that prison to be broken down and to say yes to God? Your life will never be the same as it will be more abundant than you dreamed.

Let's pray:

> *Father, thank you that you are showing us every day that our doubts can be turned into faith and courage. Help us to lean on and rely on you and keep your word centre in our lives. In Jesus' name, amen.*

CHAPTER 6

# THE PRISON OF MISSING THE MARK

Some of us can put a prison wall around our lives as we have 'missed the mark' so many times. What is that mark we are missing? It could be anything from not taking opportunities when they arose, not getting a degree when we had the chance, living our life differently from the way we thought we would or even the biggest one—not following God until later in life.

The mark is something we often set for ourselves as to what the perfect life should look like or what we should be doing in life. However, the mark in the Bible is something much more costly if we don't achieve it.

Let's look at the dictionary definition of 'mark' first. In the *Oxford Dictionary*, it means a line, figure or symbol made as an indication or record of something.

In this chapter, we will use the definition of a mark being an indication of something we should have met but didn't or a line that we should or shouldn't cross or a record of something attainable.

In Joseph's line, it doesn't appear that he missed the mark very often. He was integral in Potiphar's house and in the jail, but what about when he was younger, still in his father's house? Did he miss the mark?

I believe he did. In what way? Should Joseph have shared his dreams with his brothers or not? We know the story ended up well but was that how the story was supposed to end up? It was prophesied that the Israelites would live in Egypt. But why did Joseph have to live as a slave to be recognised? Could he have been recognised in a different way? Maybe. We will never know, but bragging about your dreams to your brothers is missing the mark.

One of the most inconspicuous stories in the Bible regarding missing the mark is Abraham's father. His story is told in a few verses at the end of Genesis 11. It states in verses 31 and 32:

> *And Terah took his son Abram and his grandson Lot, the son of Haran and his daughter in law Sarai, his son Abram's wife, and they went out with them from Ur of the Chaldeans to go to the land of Canaan; and they came to Haran and dwelt there. So, the days of Terah were two hundred and five years, and Terah died in Haran.*

There was something or someone that made Terah leave his country and go to Canaan (which was the Promised Land). But he didn't stay there—he passed through and therefore he missed the mark of where God wanted him to go. We could have been reading Terah's story and not Abraham's if he hadn't missed the mark. I wonder if in eternity he is going to regret his decision.

We need to be careful that we don't miss the mark and are obedient to God. 1 Samuel 15:22b states that to obey is better than sacrifice.

We can do the religious things for God that we think are right, e.g. going to church, reading the Bible, praying, etc., but if we are not obedient to what God calls us to do, we may as well not do those things. We are missing the mark.

Saul was another one who missed the mark in obedience and the above verse comes from the story of Saul's disobedience.

In 1 Samuel 15, Samuel told Saul that God had commanded Saul to go and fight against Amalek and wipe them out. This seems severe but it was a punishment on that nation because they ambushed God's people, the Israelites, on their way from Egypt to the Promised Land.

This seems like a simple command to a warrior and a king and was fairly straightforward. Go and annihilate Amalek—all the people, the animals and everything that breathes. It was a tough assignment but wasn't an unclear assignment.

When God gives us an assignment to do, He will make the instructions very clear to us. However, our disobedience usually stems from the fact that we consider the assignment too hard as we don't have the necessary skills and/or resources.

For Saul, his disobedience stemmed from a completely different motive. In verse 8, the Bible tells us that Saul killed everybody except for the king, who he took alive. In verse 9, the Bible tells us that Saul saved the best of the sheep, the oxen, the fatlings, the lambs and all that was good.

The motive for keeping the king alive was pride. In those days, if you could parade an enemy king through town, it was like showing off your trophy or medal for coming first place in some competition. Saul wanted to show his people how good he was and have them congratulate him to make himself feel good.

We only want to show off our wares when we are generally insecure about who we are. This is missing the mark. Everyone in the world has been created by God and we are all worth dying for. God loves each of us uniquely and we are all special to Him. We don't need to prove ourselves to God.

The motive for saving the best of the livestock is found in verse 24—Saul tells Samuel he did it because he feared the people and obeyed their voice.

Anytime we fear the voice of people over the voice of God, we are going to miss the mark. The voice of people may be louder but it's not the loudest voice we need to heed, but the voice of God. When we fear people over God, we're making them the authority over our lives and not God. We're giving them a voice that they are not entitled to have. Be careful whose voice we heed!

But who knows whether we miss the mark in a small way or a big way, it's all the same to God—we have simply missed the mark. Look at what God tells Samuel about Saul in verses 10 and 11:

> *Now the word of the Lord came to Samuel saying, "I greatly regret that I have set up Saul as king, for he has turned back from following Me, and has not performed My commandments."*

I hope I never have to hear those words from God about me, although many times I have missed the mark. I want God to be happy He has placed me in the positions that He has and not regret it one second.

Can you hear the heart and the hurt of God in these verses?

1. I greatly regret—not a little regret, but greatly.
2. Saul has turned back from following Me—Saul doesn't believe in Me and love Me.
3. Saul has not performed My commandments—Saul has disobeyed Me.

But let's go back a minute and see how Saul disobeyed:

1. He killed all the Amalekites except one. Wasn't this good enough?
2. He killed all the living things except the best ones and he didn't kill them as he wanted to sacrifice them to God (verse 21). Wasn't this a good thing?

Too often when we miss the mark, it's not because we have done anything significantly wrong, it's because of little sins.

The answer to the above questions is no. God expects full obedience to His commands because anything else is disobedience and missing the mark.

What were the consequences for Saul of missing the mark for a seemingly small disobedience?

1. He missed the mark even more later in the story. In verse 13, Saul told Samuel that 'I have performed the commandment of the Lord.' Did he? Not at all. Therefore, not only did Saul disobey God, he was now deceived into thinking he had obeyed and this deception caused him to lie.
2. He was rejected by God as king. Verse 26 tells us that Samuel spoke to him and said, 'I will not return with you, for you have rejected the word of the Lord, and the Lord has rejected you from being king over Israel.'

When we disobey God, we can mess with our calling and our destiny. Calling and destiny will only be achieved as we follow God and are obedient to Him. God has great plans for our lives, but we must obey His leading, even when it seems impossible or silly.

3. He seized the robe of Samuel in verse 27. The word 'seized' means 'take hold of suddenly and forcibly'. Saul didn't just touch Samuel's robe, he grabbed it suddenly and with some force. It was like he was trying to hold Samuel there. I'm not sure of the protocol of touching the prophet of God, but this wouldn't have been a good thing to do. By this stage, fear had taken over Saul. Samuel had just delivered a strong word and was going to depart and leave Saul standing there with no support from the prophet and no presence of God. It wasn't a nice position to be in.

4. Samuel never met with Saul again. In verse 35, it states, 'And Samuel went no more to see Saul until the day of his death. Nevertheless, Samuel mourned for Saul, and the Lord regretted that He had made Saul king over Israel.' Disobedience will take us further away from God than we ever wished to go and it will also take us further away from the people of God.

Let's recap and see what Saul's seemingly small disobedience has cost him and the steps we need to take to ensure that we don't fall into the same trap of the enemy.

> Step 1—missing the mark in one area leads to further areas of sin appearing.
>
> Step 2—we mess with our destiny and calling.
>
> Step 3—fear comes into our lives.
>
> Step 4—Christian people walk out of our lives.
>
> Step 5—the presence of God is no longer with us.

This all sounds really depressing until we remember that we now have Jesus. Jesus makes everything better and more hopeful.

We need to remember that Saul chose not to ask forgiveness for missing the mark. Was this possible in the Old Testament? Yes. How do we know? David sinned with Bathsheba and missed the mark terribly but he was repentant before God and asked God to forgive him. He still had to suffer the guilt in his heart and the consequences of his sin but God kept him as king and then even restored him later when his son tried to take over by force.

Saul had the same opportunity to own the act of missing the mark but he chose not to. What held him back and why was he different from David? It was for the same reason Saul missed the mark in the first place—fear of people. David never had a fear of people but had a complete fear of God most of the time.

How do we know Saul chose not to? Verse 30 tells us that:

> *Then he said, "I have sinned; yet honour me now,
> please, before the elders of my people and
> before Israel, and return with me, that I may
> worship the Lord your God.*

Saul was more interested in being honoured before people than repenting and being restored to the right place before God.

What about us today? If we miss the mark, what do we do? First, we must repent. 1 John 1:9 tells us:

> *If we confess our sins, He is faithful and just to forgive us our sins and to cleanse us from all unrighteousness.*

God is faithful to not only forgive our sins because of what Jesus did for us on the cross but to cleanse us from the guilt and shame of that sin. Oftentimes, there are still consequences for our sins. Sometimes, we might have to humble ourselves and ask another person to forgive us for how we spoke to them. Other times, we might have to pay a fine if we're caught speeding in our car. Sometimes, if we harbour a deep unforgiveness in our hearts towards someone, we might have to make a daily choice to forgive that person so we can then see them as God's creation instead of a bad person. The consequences can be many and varied.

If you're struggling in this area, please run to God and not away from Him. Like the father in the Prodigal Son story in Luke, God is continually looking out to see if you have turned around and are on your way back. He's waiting with His arms outstretched to welcome you. He's preparing a table before you in the presence of your enemies (Psalm 23). That table is filled with all the good things God wants to give you and impart into your life. He's ready to clothe you with His righteousness instead of the filthy rags you're currently dressed in. He wants to love you and welcome you back to His family. Only pride and fear are stopping you. Don't let them have their way. Turn back to God.

Before we go onto the next section in this chapter, let's pray:

*God, we pray and repent of the times in our lives when*
*we have missed the mark and not repented.*
*We pray that you will forgive us and cleanse us of all*
*our unrighteousness. We want to please you, God,*
*and live our lives according to Your will and plan for us.*
*Thank you for your love, mercy and grace.*
*In Jesus' name, amen.*

In the next part of this chapter, I want to discuss the fact that in missing the mark, the biggest barrier to getting free is that we can't forgive ourselves.

In the story of Joseph, we're going to have a quick look at his brothers as they struggled with forgiving themselves for selling Joseph into slavery.

This can be a big thing for us too. Often it's easier to forgive others than it is to forgive ourselves. Why is that? I believe it is because we still believe (90% of the time) that we are in control of our actions. To a certain extent that is true, but Paul makes it plain that there's a battle going on and sometimes we just miss it.

Romans 7:18–21 in the NIV is the passage where we can really see this struggle. It states:

> *For I know that in me (that is, in my flesh) nothing*
> *good dwells: for to will is present with me,*
> *but how to perform what is good I do not find.*
> *For the good that I will to do, I do not do; but the evil*
> *I will not to do, that I practice. Now if I do what I will*
> *not to do, it is no longer I who do it, but sin that dwells*
> *in me. I find then a law, that evil is present with me,*
> *the one who wills to do good. For I delight in the law of*
> *God according to the inward man.*

There is a struggle going on inside us, and when we sin against someone or even ourselves, we feel guilty and find it hard to come to Jesus to repent. Even when we do repent, we find that Satan brings that thing back to us and forgiveness seems far away.

Let's look at Joseph's brothers and their story in Genesis. I will be going back to the same story from Joseph's point of view later in the book, but I think its well worth looking at the brothers' story here.

We know they were jealous of Joseph and some of them took his coat off, threw him in a well and then sold him into slavery in Egypt. The brothers probably thought that at least they were rid of him, but consequences come from your actions, whether right or wrong.

A famine came over the whole land, including where the brothers lived. Their father told them to go to Egypt to buy grain as that was the only place that had supplies.

Joseph met them there as he was the one who had the oversight of selling the grain (Genesis 42). The brothers were treated harshly by him. Joseph locked them up in prison for three days, and then let them go. Let's look at the brothers' response to this in verse 21:

> *Then they said to one another, "We are truly guilty concerning our brother, for we saw the anguish of his soul when he pleaded with us, and we would not hear, therefore this distress has come upon us."*

The brothers were having a moment of guilt over what they'd done. The consequences were starting to be apparent in their lives.

Joseph ended up giving them grain and sending them on their way but made them promise to bring their younger brother next time or else they would not be served.

It took a long time for their father to agree to send Benjamin back with them but finally they went (Genesis 43). This time when they came back, Joseph prepared a dinner for them. He again sent them away but this time, he tricked them with a stolen cup to make them return. In verse 16 of chapter 44, the brothers again felt guilty for what had transpired by Joseph being sold into slavery. It states (in part):

> *"Or how shall we clear ourselves? God has found out the iniquity of your servants: here we are, my lord's slaves, both we and he also with whom the cup was found."*

Hang on, wasn't the cup found in Benjamin's sack? Why then did they say God 'found out the iniquity of your servants'? The brothers were wallowing in so much guilt and shame they couldn't get their facts right.

Genesis 45 is my favourite part of Joseph's story. It's when he reveals himself to his brothers and forgives them for their part in his journey to Egypt. In verse 8, it states:

> *"So now it was not you who sent me here, but God; and He has made me a father to Pharaoh, and lord of all his house, and a ruler throughout all the land of Egypt..."*

From that encounter, all was seemingly forgiven, or was it? For Joseph, that was the end of the matter. However, the brothers still couldn't forgive themselves and struggled with this unforgiveness until their father died.

In Genesis 50:15–21, the brothers again came to Joseph. Now remember, at this stage, they had all been occupying the same land for a number of years so their interactions would have been many.

In verse 15, the brothers said to each other, 'Perhaps Joseph will hate us and may actually repay us for all the evil which we did to him.' Unforgiveness of themselves was still in their hearts many years later.

In verse 19, Joseph replies to his brothers, 'Do not be afraid, for am I in the place of God?' In verse 21 it states that he comforted them and spoke kindly to them.

Finally, Joseph's brothers were free from holding unforgiveness over themselves. How do I know that? The Bible does not record any further exchanges on this subject.

I think we should all remember Joseph's words to his brothers—am I in the place of God? If Jesus died on the cruel cross for our sins, who are we to hold unforgiveness towards ourselves?

In Psalm 103:11–12, it states:

> *For as the heavens are high above the earth,*
> *so great is His mercy toward those who fear Him.*
> *As far as the east is from the west, so far has*
> *He removed our transgressions from us.*

Can you even see the far east to the far west with your eyes? No, you can't or else you would be looking across oceans. The east never meets the west and vice versa. That means that our sins are so far removed from us that they are unsearchable. We can't find them and bring them back, nor can we throw them any further away.

Corrie ten Boom had a saying where sins had been forgiven—they are in the ocean and there is no fishing allowed. This is for others' sins as well as our own.

Forgive yourself and walk in the light, where God wants us to walk. Unforgiveness causes us to walk in darkness. It's time to turn the light back on so others can see Jesus in you.

Let's pray:

> *Father, we* **thank** *you that Jesus died on the cross for our sins. We ask, Father, that you continually remind us that once we repent of our sins, they are as far away from us as the east is from the west. We forgive ourselves and repent before you of where we are still holding on to past sins. Thank you for your forgiveness. In Jesus' name, amen.*

CHAPTER 7

# REJECTION

Rejection is a word that connotates a painful feeling. We have all felt the pain of rejection in some form or another. For some of us, we can move past it or just 'shrug it off'. For others of us, rejection is deeply implanted within us due to circumstances beyond our control. It's because we can't control rejection, so we struggle with it.

In the *Oxford Dictionary*, 'rejection', in relation to people, means the actions of spurning a person's affections. When we reject someone, we push them away. We can do this deliberately so the person knows it or we can do it deliberately so the person somehow feels it.

Rejection generally has nothing to do with the person experiencing the rejection and everything to do with the perpetrator. How can I say this? We push people away because we either don't like what they're doing to us, or we don't like how they could change our lives, or we don't like how they are living their lives. It is all about self. Rejecting someone deep down is being scared of change or changing.

We reject our spouse and apply for divorce because they do something to us. It could be that we are the guilty party and have been having an affair or that they are not behaving the way we would like.

I have personal experience with rejection. I was adopted as a baby. My mother didn't hold me or tell me she loved me. She had determined in her heart that she wasn't going to keep me. Throughout the pregnancy, there was no love, only rejection. This impacted my life for many years.

I was adopted into my family and three years later, they had their own daughter. Even though I was loved, I felt rejected. I didn't look like them or even think like them.

Because of my rejection issues, I rejected others. I allowed very few people close to me as I was afraid that they were going to hurt me or if they knew the real me, they would reject me.

Rejection is a cycle. I was rejected, so I rejected others.

It wasn't until my first son was born that I had the sense I wasn't going to be rejected again. He needed me and, in some way, I needed him too. He taught me how to love and how to not feel rejected.

My first husband and I divorced, and I was left alone with my two boys. It was a time when I gained confidence in myself and knew that whatever happened, I could do it, with God. I had given my heart to God a few years earlier. Without Him, I don't think I would have done as well.

A few years later, I met and married my now husband. He had so much belief in me and made me feel loved and accepted and after a few years, rejection no longer had a hold on me.

Rejection can only be overcome by knowing the love of your creator, God, and feeling safe and secure with others. Rejection is a security issue.

Do I still struggle with it? Yes, at times, but it is at those times that I remind myself that God loves me and so does my family. Whatever others think of me is their perspective and may not be truth. This has helped greatly.

Back to our story of Joseph. I believe that this is one of the major issues that Joseph struggled with in his earlier years. His mother died—the only one who could have offered him the love and security he needed. His father tried, but his attempts only drove the wedge further between Joseph and his brothers.

Once Rachel died, Joseph and baby Benjamin were her only descendants. Jacob was their father, but he had a whole other family to be there for. Leah would have been instructed by Jacob to provide care for Joseph and Benjamin, which she possibly resented. I am using poetic licence here as the Bible does not talk about these details.

However, we can see the results. Leah's sons hated Joseph and so did Jacob's concubines' sons. This hatred would have been passed down long before there was a coat of many colours. The rejection that ensued in Joseph's life from his brothers was not the result of anything he did but was the result of love not being spread. Love will always override rejection eventually.

When Jacob made Joseph the coat of many colours, it made his brothers hate him more, but it didn't start the hate. Hatred of people will always lead to us rejecting them. We see this in our world today. This particular group hates that particular group because they disagree and then they 'cancel' them out.

I am unsure how you can cancel people when they are still alive. When a concert is cancelled, it means it is not going ahead. But when we cancel people, it doesn't mean they cease to exist.

Hatred led to the rejection of Joseph, which then led to the brothers devising a scheme to get rid of him. Sometimes, we can reject others so much that they no longer exist in our world. This is not the way God wants us to treat others. God said to love others.

When Joseph was sold and went to Egypt, he must have felt so much rejection from his brothers. However, he didn't drown in it and let it define him, he looked to God for a new definition for his life.

If you feel rejected by someone, it's time to seek God and let Him define you. God never defines anybody as 'rejected'. He defines them by 'child of God', 'accepted', 'son or daughter of the King', 'loved by God', 'masterpiece', etc. It's time to receive your identity from God and not from fallen man.

When Joseph was purchased in Egypt as a slave, he ensured that his new master prospered, which he did. When he was put in prison, he ensured the prison 'prospered'. It was because of these actions that God then prospered him, which we will look at later in the book.

What strategies can we use so we can also be free of rejection?

The first one is to make sure that we are right with God. The enemy can only succeed in speaking negative things over our lives if we don't have Jesus. Of course, the enemy can still speak over our lives, but with Jesus, we can renew our minds and start to think differently, not only about others but about ourselves.

Jacob could only come back to his brother, Esau, who rejected him, after he had had an encounter with God. The story begins in Genesis 32:1. Before, we look at that story, let's recap a bit of Jacob's story. He had been sent away by his parents because he had stolen not only Esau's birthright but also his blessing from a dying father.

In those days, these were more important than money or wealth. The birthright ensured that the firstborn received 50% of the inheritance and the rest of the siblings had the other 50% divided between them. With respect to the blessing of the father, these people understood what we fail to understand today—words are really important. A blessing spoken over you guaranteed you had something to reflect on and believe in when the times were tough. A blessing that was always believed guaranteed you were prosperous in all you did. The word spoken was very important. Why?

In Genesis 1, God set this principal in place. God spoke and things happened exactly as He spoke. Words are the seeds of faith spoken, either good or bad. Good to remember for all of us!

Jacob stealing the birthright and the blessing was a big deal and the only way Esau could get them back was by killing Jacob. Jacob's parents sent him away to his mother's brother, Laban, in a far-off land.

Jacob was not treated well by Laban but through that experience, he became a better man. After 20 years, Jacob decided to return home with his wives, children and his goods. But to do that, he needed to send messengers to Esau to advise him he was on his way.

In verse 6 of Genesis 32, Esau sent messengers back stating that he was on his way. This sent fear and distress into Jacob (verse 7), so he devised a plan to split everything into groups so if Esau attacked, the others could get away.

This was a natural solution to a supernatural issue. Rejection can't be dealt with in a natural way. It won't work. It must be defeated by the power of God.

In verse 24 of chapter 32, Jacob was all alone on one side of the ford of Jabbok whilst his family was on the other side. A Man wrestled with Jacob all night long. This was a physical wrestling, but it was more than that—it was also a spiritual wrestling.

To get rejection out of our lives, there will need to be a physical wrestling, where we speak 'life' over ourselves, as well as a spiritual wrestling, where we wrestle that thing out of our lives. It can't be cast out; it must be wrestled through.

The Man told Jacob to let him go as the day was breaking but Jacob stated, 'Not until you bless me.' Rejection requires a blessing at the end of the wrestling.

Have a look at verse 28, where the Man answers Jacob. It states:

> *And He said, "Your name shall no longer be called Jacob, but Israel: for you have struggled with God and with men, and have prevailed."*

The name Jacob means 'deceiver', but one of the definitions of the name Israel means 'prince with God'[4]. God changes our name 'rejection' to son or daughter of God. As a son or daughter of God, we are never rejected because God promises that He will never leave us or forsake us. That is a good anti-rejection promise to remember.

Let's have a look at the meaning of 'struggled' in that verse. The primary root of the Hebrew word used here is 'prevail'. It means having power over. Jacob struggled with rejection from God and man until he prevailed over it. This means that to be free from rejection means it's a fight. It will not go easily but from continuing to read the story of Jacob's

---

[4] Definition of Hebrew Names: Israel | AHRC (ancient-hebrew.org)

life from this point on, his life is so different. He no longer deceives but seems to have a different attitude.

Rejection no longer has a hold because he prevailed over it.

The second strategy is to know who you are in God. This has been touched on above, but I want to look at the story of Esther to see how this can be applied to our lives.

In Esther 2, we meet Esther for the first time. The first story is the back chapter of how Esther found herself in the situation she did.

In verses 5 and 6, we get the backstory of Mordecai, who was Esther's cousin. He was a Jew from the tribe of Benjamin. He had been carried away into captivity from Jerusalem to the kingdom of Babylon, where he now found himself. Mordecai brought up Esther (his uncle's daughter), for her parents had died.

Esther was lovely and beautiful, and Mordecai had brought her up as his own daughter (verse 7).

That is all the Bible tells us but let's use some poetic licence to see what Esther may have been feeling. Here she was, a young girl—an orphan. She was not yet married so must have been a teenager or a little older at this point.

Her parents had died. Without her uncle taking her in, who knows what would have happened to her? This young girl probably grieved so much for her parents (there don't seem to be any siblings on the scene). She would have questioned why they died and would have felt very rejected at this point. Although Mordecai would have done his best, we don't know what his family looked like either. Did he have a wife and children or was he only a bit older than Esther? We don't know the answers to these questions, but the story further on may give us some clues.

The king was looking for a new wife as he had ousted his old wife (Esther 1). The call went out for young, beautiful women to be gathered to the palace to be given beauty preparations and then go to the king to be deemed if they were suitable or not. This sounds like a great plan if you were deemed suitable. If you were not deemed suitable, because you have probably slept with the king, you were then relegated to the harem where you would spend the rest of your life on call, waiting for the king.

Esther joined the other young women in this endeavour to find the king a new wife. Why did she do that? Did she willingly go along with the plan even knowing what the end of her life might look like? Was this a good deal anyway as she would be looked after by someone else her entire life? Was there no man among the Jewish people that was more suitable for her? I am sure these questions and more would have been going through her mind. Was this just another time of rejection added on by her cousin Mordecai or did she willingly go?

What sometimes looks like rejection in our lives is actually God's perfect plan for our lives. What we are feeling is probably not the end of our story.

Esther had to complete 12 months of beauty preparations before she went into the king. This was a long time to wait and think about the path before you. However, her time came, and she went into the king and the king loved her and made her his queen. Esther now lived in the palace away from family. It was a perfect time to ponder and let that rejection go deeper. But did that happen? No, it didn't because Esther found favour with all in the palace as she knew who she was in God. Mordecai told her not to reveal her heritage but even though she doesn't reveal it, it doesn't mean she forgot it.

Even when others don't know who we are and Who we serve, we shouldn't forget.

But when we know Whose we are there may come a time when we will be tested. The time came for Esther when Haman devised a wicked plot to destroy the Jews and received the king's consent.

Once Esther found out, her response was not, 'Oh no! I am a Jew, I need to do something.' Her response was to hide as she feared being rejected and then killed by the king. She had not been called to go into the king for a month and if she went when he didn't call, she risked being killed (chapter 4:11).

Mordecai came back with an answer that we all love to quote but for Esther, it was a call to remember Whose she was in a situation that could have been fatal. The quote is found in chapter 4:13–14:

> *And Mordecai told them to answer Esther: "Do not think in your heart you will escape in the king's palace any more than all the other Jews. For if you remain*

> *completely silent at this time, relief and deliverance will arise for the Jews from another place, but you and your father's house will perish. Yet who knows whether you have come to the kingdom for such a time as this?"*

Rejection will have us forgetting who we are and hiding in the corner. We need a Mordecai in our lives to remind us of who we are and Whose we are. This statement was a turning point in Esther's life. No longer could she hide her fears of who she really was, but she also couldn't hide her heritage or her beliefs.

What did she do? She fasted and prayed for three days. In that time, God would have reminded her that she was not only a wife of the king in the natural, but she was a daughter of the king in the spiritual. He would have reminded her that He went before her and was with her. When everyone else couldn't or wouldn't walk with her, He would. That is great for us to remember when we are struggling with rejection. Rejection always comes when we feel left out, like we are the only ones missing out on whatever it is. People may leave us out, but God never will.

You can keep reading the story if you never have but in a few sentences, Esther goes into the king and he is pleased to see her. She invites him and Haman for lunch twice and then reveals who she is. The king is not happy and puts Haman to death and issues a new decree. The Jewish people end up victorious, Esther stays as queen and Mordecai is promoted to a palace position.

If we let rejection rule our lives, we will never fulfil the perfect plan that God has for our lives. We will hide in the corner and when we stand before God, our excuses won't work. Rejection is a hard taskmaster that keeps us bound to people and not to God. It's an idol in our lives that keeps our fear of people more prevalent in our lives than the fear of God.

Like Esther, it's time to fast and pray to get rid of that rejection and let God speak into our lives what only He can.

The third strategy is to find our calling from God and walk in it. For this strategy, I'm going to continue my own story.

For many years I struggled in this area, and it was only recently (in my mid-fifties) that I really understood the call of God on my life. Once I had, I could celebrate other people's giftings without thinking that something was wrong with me.

Some people are blessed and find their calling from God early in their lives. Others have never felt the continual sting of rejection in their lives so whether they are walking in their calling or not, they seem to be content. Some others always say, 'I don't care what people think.' That is a front and probably not what is really going on in their hearts.

For us Christians, sometimes we are told to try things and see if they resonate with us. This is what I did (and it's a good idea). Some of those things were:

1. Children's church or Sunday school—very soon, I realised I didn't have what it takes to be a teacher of children in Sunday school. It was a struggle for me

to come up with lesson plans that I thought would be engaging but probably weren't. Generally, children are not drawn to me either, so it was not a good idea for me to continue down this path.

2. Creative team or involved in the music—this seemed like a good idea as I had played piano for many years when I was younger and liked music. However, changing from piano notes to chords did not bode well as I haven't had a lot of success with rhythm. Singing is definitely not my strong point either—I just make a joyful noise.

3. Giving messages in church—this was something I enjoyed and I felt I was good at. Even though message writing came fairly easily to me, it wasn't where God wanted me. I generally did one message and wasn't asked again. This could have had something to do with character development as well; I'm not sure. But it was a stepping stone for me to know which direction I should take (not that it was in a local church setting).

What happened in my story? When I was 47, God told me to write a blog and call it 'Living the life God intended'. I wondered what a blog was and thought that nobody was going to read it. But I was obedient and started it in January 2015. It's not overly successful, but it's small and it's still going. I have learned that God doesn't measure success by the number of followers I have but by my obedience. If you have a small church of 100 people or 10,000 people, as long as you are obedient, you will still hear the words, 'Well done, good and faithful servant.' This is the same as my blog. If I'm obedient, I will have the favour and blessing of God.

God then told me to write a book. Truth be told, I had had this desire in my heart for a long time. It was something God planted there back in my twenties.

But of course, I argued with God. My arguments consisted of the fact that writing was my weakest skill at work, nobody was going to read it, how did I start, I didn't know anyone who did this, etc., etc. Seven years later, in 2022, I released my first book and this one is my second.

I have joined Omega Writers, which is for Australian Christian writers and am now a part of their committee. God has gone before me in this aspect and made it possible.

I'm walking in my calling as a teacher of the Word of God through books and a blog. I'm content in God and no longer suffer with rejection. Why? Because I'm in my lane, totally loved by God, loved by my family and friends and best of all, I'm walking in obedience to what God has called me to do.

What is your calling from God and are you walking in it? It will be another strategy to get you over rejection and I promise it will work. It worked for me and will work for you.

In closing, if you have rejection in your life, admit it and bring it to God. Allow Him to heal you through his love. Know that you are totally loved by God. If you don't have a relationship with God, at the back of this book, there's a tool to help you. That decision will be the best one you can make and will set you on the path to freedom.

Once you know this, seek God for your particular calling. Everyone has one, whether it's big or small. If you are obedient to God, you will be fulfilled. I would encourage you to read Jeremiah 29:11, write it down, memorise it and then start walking in it. God has an amazing plan for your life and it doesn't include rejection.

Let's pray:

> *Father, thank you that you love us so dearly. Thank you for your perfect plan that enables us to choose You. Thank you that you never reject us and you continue to walk with us. I pray that You will reveal the particular calling You have over each person's life. May they know it and walk in it. In Jesus' name, amen.*

CHAPTER 8

# PRISON OF SHAME

Shame. Most of us think this is something that will forever be around our lives, and keeps us safe from people and not a prison to escape from. Why do we carry around shame this way? If we released it, we would have to deal with not only the thing causing the shame but our reactions to people. Shame tells us to hide away from others. God tells us to love others.

What is the meaning of shame? In the *Oxford Dictionary*, 'shame' means a painful feeling of humiliation or distress caused by the consciousness of wrong or foolish behaviour. Shame can either be caused by others or caused by us. Shame caused by others is usually when they have violated us in some sort of physical way. Shame caused by us is generally caused by our own actions, thoughts or words.

What about Joseph's life up to this point in our story? He possibly felt shame as a young boy as he didn't have his mother.

This may be why he acted tough in front of his brothers, telling them of his dreams. He tattled on his brothers if they did something wrong.

Shame can cause us to hurt others in the same way we are hurting on the inside. I believe the biggest test of Joseph's shame came when he was sold as a slave and later put in prison for a crime he didn't commit. Both of these things would cause that painful feeling of humiliation. Let's consider them separately.

Joseph belonged to the family of Jacob and was one of his sons. This was the family God had chosen to be His people through Abraham. It would have felt very special to be a part of that family. Joseph's dad Jacob had much wealth as well—lots of livestock and other animals. He would have lived a very privileged life, even though they all had to work hard.

Then came the day when his brothers' hatred for him turned into something more sinister. It was the day they stripped him of his robe, threw him in a well and sold him to the slave traders for money. Imagine selling your brother or sister for money. Joseph's life, to his brothers, was worth 20 shekels of silver, which equates to about $200 in our currency today. That was a lot of money back then.

He was then put up on the slave trader's blocks and sold to the highest bidder. The highest bidder was Potiphar. Imagine the shame that Joseph felt standing on those slave trader's blocks. His brothers had determined his worth at 20 shekels of silver and now someone else was going to determine his worth. It would have been humiliating and painful for him and would have caused him much distress. Shame would have been coupled with rejection and doubt about the dreams God had given him.

What was Joseph's reaction to this shame? Normally, when shame gets around us, we get anxious, want to avoid people and just hide. But what did Joseph do? The next verse after the one where Joseph is sold in Genesis 39:1 states that:

*The Lord was with Joseph, and he was a successful man.*

Hang on, didn't Joseph just come through the pitfalls of shame in his life? Yes, he did, but he didn't let shame define him. He recognised that who others said he was, was not who God said he was. From here on, we can see Joseph putting his whole trust in God.

Joseph served Potiphar so well that he was made overseer of his whole house. This was not the attribute of a man holding shame. We don't see Joseph getting anxious, hiding away or avoiding people. He put that shame aside and decided to prosper in this man's household. Shame will always go when it's exposed and released.

Was this the end of Joseph's shame journey? It seems it should have been. Joseph passed the test with flying colours.

But it wasn't the end. Shame fights hard to stay in our lives and will use whatever situations it can to bring it to the surface so we don't prosper but retreat.

Potiphar's wife decided that Joseph looked like a man she needed. She was probably used to getting her own way. After all, she had a houseful of servants that did her bidding. But this was one request that was never going to be met. Maybe the man who held the position previously had succumbed to her wishes. We are not told.

With Joseph, however, she met her match. He was not going to succumb to her wishes no matter what. He understood what his rights were and his master's rights, and he was never going to cross that line. So he declined her invitations. We don't have to accept every invitation we are given.

She tricked him and told lies about Joseph and he was thrown into prison. Shame had again taken hold of his life. He was the overseer of Potiphar's house, who was an officer of Pharaoh and a captain of the guard. His position was really important. Now Joseph found himself a prisoner in the king's prison.

Shame again tested him. The prison was the perfect place to hide, withdraw from people and become anxious. But did Joseph succumb to shame's attributes?

In verses 21–23 of chapter 39 of Genesis, we read the following:

> *But the Lord was with Joseph and showed him mercy, and He gave him favour in the sight of the keeper of the prison. And the keeper of the prison committed to Joseph's hand all the prisoners who were in the prison; whatever they did there, it was his doing. The keeper of*

*the prison did not look into anything that was under Joseph's authority, because the Lord was with him; and whatever he did, the Lord made it prosper.*

I love what the first sentence states above. It states that the Lord was with Joseph and showed him mercy. When Joseph was sold into Potiphar's house, it only states that the Lord was with Joseph. Now it states that the Lord was not only with him but showed him mercy.

The word 'mercy' in Hebrew is *checed* and means 'kindness'. God was kind towards Joseph in the prison. It was the kindness of God that put Joseph in the prison. What do I mean by that? If Joseph had stayed in Potiphar's house even as the lowest servant, the temptation to sin with Potiphar's wife might have become too strong and he might have succumbed.

Further, it was in prison that Pharaoh found him. If Joseph had not been in the prison, Pharaoh might never have found him, and his life and the life of his family would have been changed forever.

Kindness always defeats shame. When we understand that kindness is a power, we will use it more often. Kindness is often seen as weakness, but it's really a strength in our own lives and those it touches.

There were many people with shame whose stories are told in the Bible and we are going to look at a few and see what they did to overcome shame or who touched their lives and enabled them to overcome shame.

The first person in the Bible that comes to mind when I speak of shame is Paul the apostle. You might think that he's a strange person to have a battle with shame, but I think he would have, and it's confirmed in a roundabout way in the Bible.

Generally, we feel shame because of our past. Shame dwells in our present because of things we have done or said or that others have done to us. Shame is only in our future when the future turns into today.

Before Paul (who was originally called Saul) was converted in Acts 9, we read of his involvement in the death of the first martyr after Jesus. That man's name was Stephen. Let's review the story in Acts 7:51 to 8:1.

Stephen had been addressing the high priest and the others in the council. But in verses 51 and 52 of Acts, Stephen starts rebuking the people listening and the people were cut to the heart. Instead of repenting, they grew angry, cast him out of the council, took him outside the city and stoned him. He was the first martyr of the new Christian church.

The ones who were stoning him laid their clothes at the feet of a young man named Saul (verse 58). But did this affect Saul (later known as Paul)? No, as in verse 1 of the next chapter, it states that 'Saul was consenting to his death.'

Saul had not yet had his Damascus experience so was still a Jew and a very fervent one for the law of the Jews. How do we know this? In chapter 9 verse 1 of Acts it states:

> *Then Saul, still breathing threats and murder against the disciples of the Lord, went to the high priest and*

> *asked letters from him to the synagogues of Damascus,*
> *so that if he found any who were of the Way, whether*
> *men or women, he might bring them bound to*
> *Jerusalem.*

Saul didn't care who he was persecuting. He was so angry that they were not now following the Law of Moses. Shame can impact our future when we or others do or say something that's not understood.

So how did these recorded events and possibly many others lead to shame being part of Paul's life?

1 Corinthians 15:9–10 give us some insight. The verses state:

> *For I am the least of all the apostles, who am not*
> *worthy to be called an apostle, because I persecuted*
> *the church of God. But by the grace of God, I am what*
> *I am, and His grace toward me was not in vain; but I*
> *have laboured more abundantly than they all, yet not I,*
> *but the grace of God, which was with me.*

In the first part of that verse, shame is speaking. Can you hear it? I am the least and I am not worthy because... This is shame speaking and it happens to those of us who hold onto it.

Shame tells us that we need to continue holding onto our past as if it's some sort of penitence we have to hold onto for the rest of our lives. Shame never lets us forget who we were—*were*, not *are*. Shame always makes us remember the bad and not the good.

The shame of being a single mother gripped me for many years. I gave my life to Jesus one year after my son was born. But because of who I was at the time, even the church judged me. It told me the only way out was to get married to the father of my child (who had also recently been saved). Shame was not something to be forgiven then and worked out with God, it was a natural response to circumstances.

If we do something in our lives to alleviate shame, such as pay back all the ones we stole from or get married, then we will never be free. It's only when we do what Paul did in the next part of the above passage that we will be set free.

It's only by the grace of God coming in once we repent of our sins, surrounding the shame, that we will be free. We may remember those circumstances, but they won't have a hold over us. Satan will try and use them to bring us down but because we know who we are in God, we can refute his attacks. The grace of God means being empowered to prosper. Being prosperous in our lives does not equate with living in shame but standing above and against that thing until it disappears and is defeated. Shame is a spirit and can be defeated by Jesus.

One thing I noticed in the verse above is that because Paul persecuted the church, he laboured more abundantly to see people won to Jesus. Another way we can defeat shame in our lives is to overcome in the area where we feel shame. Being a single mum, I labour to help other single mums feel loved, supported and not judged. I am labouring in the area of shame so that its power can no longer be seen and felt.

Another tactic Paul used to defeat shame in his life is found in Philippians 3:13. It states in part b:

> *But one thing I do, forgetting those things which are behind, and reaching forward to those things which are ahead, I press toward the goal for the prize of the upward call of God in Christ Jesus.*

Paul was stating that he forgets what is behind him. This is a deliberate action on his part. I don't know about you, but I find it hard to forget some things that have happened in my life.

That word 'forgetting' in Greek means to 'lose out of mind' or 'to neglect'. Have you ever thought about neglecting those old negative thoughts? 'Neglecting' means not giving any attention to. What Paul is saying in those verses is that he neglected those things that were behind and reached forward to those things he needed to pay attention to.

We can deal with shame in the same way. Shame always has to do with our past. It never has anything to do with today or with our future. We may do something today and feel shame, but we know to repent and ask forgiveness for it and move on. This is different from the stronghold of shame that comes from our past.

We need to neglect it, to not give any attention to it. If we do that, it will go away. So how do we neglect shame when it comes back to trouble us? By thinking about all of the good things that might have come out of that shame. For me, it was becoming a mum and knowing that, unlike my story, my baby was going to know his mum and we would grow together. This young boy taught me to love and be loved. I am so grateful for this experience.

Shame can be broken over our lives by first repenting of the thing that caused it and receiving God's forgiveness, then neglecting any thought about it when it tries to overwhelm us.

The next story I want to look at with regard to shame is Peter. Peter was a disciple of Jesus and had walked with Him for about three and a half years when his shame incident occurred.

First, let's look at some poetic justice with Peter. Peter was cleaning his nets one day when Jesus came by and asked to use Peter's boat for ministry. After He had finished speaking, He told Peter to cast down his nets for a catch. Peter argued with Jesus, but Jesus won. (Remember this statement—you will never win an argument with Jesus. I know because I have tried.) Peter pulled in so many fish, he had to get his partners in the other boats to help him. He then fell before Jesus and told Jesus he was a sinful man. Did that bother Jesus? No, because His response to Peter was, 'Do not be afraid. From now on, you will catch men.' Peter left all to follow Jesus (Luke 5:1–11).

Peter knew who he was when Jesus called him but that didn't stop Peter from following Jesus. Over the next couple of years, Peter assisted Jesus with ministry, saw many healed and demons cast out, had all his needs met and was one of the top three disciples. In an environment like this, most of us would have thought that Jesus would rub off on us and something as dire as shame would not touch us. Wrong! Just because we are a Christian does not mean that the enemy has ceased to attack. Satan always attacks us in our weakest areas. If shame is or was one of yours, you will be attacked with it even though you have given your life to Jesus. However, there is a way through it that means you win.

Let's look at Peter's 'shame' moment. It happened as the Last Supper was finishing. Jesus and the disciples had shared the Passover meal and Judas had left to betray Jesus. Jesus shared His last words with His disciples, and they should have been paying attention (except that at the time they didn't know these were his last words).

Jesus had just taught the new commandment in John 13:34. Verse 36 is where our story begins.

Peter asked Jesus where He was going. Only a few verses earlier, Jesus had told them that he would only be with them a little while longer. Jesus told Peter that where He was going, Peter couldn't come now but would join him later. Those words would have conjured up all types of scenarios in my brain, especially the thought of why I couldn't go.

Peter had the same thought. In verse 37, he continued with these words, 'I will lay down my life for Your sake.' This was a big statement. Sometimes we make big statements to

God as well. For example, I will pray for one hour each day; each person I come across, I will speak with them about Jesus; I will fast one day each week, etc.

Jesus knows that it may be impossible for us at the time as it was for Peter. But that was in the future.

Jesus spoke to Peter and stated, 'The rooster will not crow till you have denied me three times.' Roosters only crow in the morning and it was now night. Jesus was saying before morning comes, in a few short hours, you will tell others three times that you don't know me personally at all.

Sometimes in our lives, we want to do big things for Jesus, but Jesus is continually reminding us of the next steps today or tomorrow. For example, how are you going to treat people? How are you going to speak? Are you going to trust me? Do you know I love you and have your best interests at heart? Jesus wants us to walk step by step and then eventually those big things will come if they are in God's plan for our lives.

To find out how this story ends, we need to go over to John 18:15. But before we do, let's backtrack a little. Once the Passover was finished, Jesus and his disciples went to the Garden of Gethsemane. There Jesus taught them and then he went off to pray. Jesus knew what was coming and needed strength from God to go through it, as it was His cup to bear. Peter, James and John were asked to pray with Jesus, but they kept falling asleep. Then Jesus was arrested and taken away.

Peter and another disciple followed at a distance (whilst the others fled) and was standing around the fire warming himself.

The servant girl asked Peter in verse 17 if he was one of Jesus' disciples and Peter answered, 'No.' Again, he was asked the same question by those who stood around the fire and again by one of the servants of the high priest and he again said no to both of them (verses 25–27). After the third time, the rooster crowed, and the words Jesus spoke came to pass.

In Luke 22:61–62, it states:

> *And the Lord turned and looked at Peter. Then Peter remembered the word of the Lord... So, Peter went out and wept bitterly.*

The shame of his foolish actions at that time would have been hard to bear. Jesus had done so much for Peter and in saying 'no' three times, Peter had denied he knew Jesus, whom he absolutely loved.

This shame was in Peter's life for a number of days, and he probably derided himself constantly over that time. He heard about Jesus being crucified and realised that the last encounter they'd had was the look Jesus gave him after he had denied him.

This is how we can be sometimes. We do or say something shameful and then cry bitterly over it, but it doesn't change the fact that we feel embarrassment and are embarrassed in front of that particular person or group of people. Embarrassment is the feeling of shame in our lives.

So what did Peter eventually do? In John 21:3, Peter tells the others he is going fishing. He is going back to the things he knew before shame hit him. Oftentimes we think that doing something we used to do before the shame moment will help us forget the shame or that somehow the years will evaporate into thin air. They won't be a memory; they just won't have ever happened.

However, Jesus just doesn't leave anyone in shame, especially those who are His sons and daughters. Jesus comes to restore Peter. In John 21:15–19, Jesus asks Peter three questions to counteract those three denials.

The three questions were all very similar—does Peter love Jesus? This is the key to recovering from shame—restoration of the relationship, where possible. If it's not physically possible, then restore the relationship in your heart—forgiving the other person or people.

However, the three restoration responses Jesus gives to Peter regarding his shame are quite different.

As stated before, shame keeps us locked in the past. To restore us from shame, we need to have our future spoken over us.

The three responses were 'feed my lambs', 'tend my sheep' and 'feed my sheep'. In essence, Jesus was saying, 'Peter, your future is in me and it is in my ministry through you. I have shown you how to feed the lambs and tend and feed the sheep and now I am handing it over to you. It's now your responsibility to take this forward.'

If you are living with shame today, it's time to repent of it, to love the people involved in that situation and walk into the glorious future God has for you.

Shame can be defeated, and you can walk in victory knowing you are a child of God and you are righteous through Him and loved by Him.

Let's pray:

*Father, we thank you that you have forgiven us of all the shame areas in our lives. Please help us to forgive those we have wronged or who have wronged us in this shame situation. Thank you, God, that you have a great plan for our lives, and we are walking in it step by step every day. So grateful to you, God. Amen."*

CHAPTER 9

# JOSEPH IN THE PALACE

The story of Joseph was paused at the end of Genesis 39 where Joseph was now in prison. We then looked at some of the prisons that we can find ourselves in—not physical prisons like Joseph's, but emotional prisons. However, if you find yourself in a physical prison then the learnings from Joseph's life are the same that you should follow once you become a Christian—a follower of Jesus.

The last verse in Genesis 39 (verse 23) is for all of us. It states in the NIV Bible:

> *The keeper of the prison did not look into*
> *anything that was under Joseph's authority,*
> *because the Lord was with him; and whatever he did,*
> *the Lord made it prosper.*

This is how we should be living whilst in our prisons—remembering that the Lord is with us. Then the things we do for Him in that season of life will prosper.

Even though God was with Joseph in the prison, this was not where he was meant to be forever. Prisons are not meant as forever places. They are meant as places to build character and our relationship with God so that we can move on from there and impact people's lives for good.

Prison for most of us is not a life sentence (unless we were put there in the natural by a judge or we keep ourselves there). The plans of God for our lives that Jeremiah 29:11 speaks about are for good. Prison is not generally a good place so therefore, God has something more in store for us. It's time to be freed from our prison and get to work following God and His good plan for our lives.

Genesis 40 is where the story takes a turn; not a dramatic one but there is a turn there. The story does not directly deal with Joseph, but the stories here have an impact on Joseph's future. Often it's in helping others through their trials that we discover what we are really meant to be doing.

The two men involved in this story are the butler and the baker of the king of Egypt. They both offended the king. The Bible doesn't tell us how but to offend the king was serious business. We also need to be careful we don't offend the king—our leaders in all capacities—or we could find ourselves where these men went.

These two men were put in prison. Sometimes, our own prisons can be caused by offence or by not honouring where the Bible commands us too.

Guess who was put over these men? Joseph. Let's think about this for a minute. These men were servants of the king and when they were put in prison, they were no longer servants but prisoners and their leader was another prisoner. If they had offended the king, how easy would it be to offend their prison leader, as he was lower in rank than the king? Be careful in our own lives that we don't consider ourselves too good for others, as it could be those others that help us!

In verse 5 of chapter 40, it states that both the butler and the baker each had a dream one night. The next morning, Joseph came in and noticed they were sad. He asked them about it, and they told him they'd each had a dream and couldn't interpret it.

Isn't this so like God? He ministers to others, even in our prison, through the gifts He has placed on our lives. Who better to interpret dreams than Joseph? Hang on, it had been years since Joseph had had his own dreams. Did he really have the ability to help these men out? Yes, he did. Gifts don't expire—they are given to us by God for good.

In verse 8, Joseph makes an amazing statement to them. He said, 'Do not interpretations belong to God? Tell them to me please.'

My question is, did these men know who God was or did they think it was Joseph? I am not sure they really comprehended that statement. They were just happy that someone or even a god could help them.

The butler went first and then the baker. The butler's dream was favourable in that he was restored to his position and the baker's dream wasn't in that he was put to death.

Joseph not only interpreted their dreams correctly, but he also made this statement to the butler in verse 14:

> *"But remember me when it is well with you, and please show kindness to me; make mention of me to Pharaoh, and get me out of this house.*

Joseph's hopes for release had now risen—he had an advocate on Pharaoh's staff. But alas, it states in verse 23 that 'The chief butler did not remember Joseph but forgot him.'

When we try to get out of prison using man's way, it won't work. We need to do it God's way and in God's timing. All Joseph could see were prison walls, but all God could see was character building for a man who would bring glory to His Name and speak God's name in Pharaoh's court. A man who would become second in charge in Egypt.

God's ways are always higher than our ways and His thoughts are greater than our thoughts. Most times, we think God's timing is not right, but it's always perfect as God knew what would happen in the nation of Egypt whereas we have a vision of self-preservation.

At this stage, Joseph was probably wondering how or if he would ever get out but his time was coming. God doesn't work on our character because he intends to leave us in the same place. God has promotion and increase on His mind for us, but it's on His terms and not ours.

Between chapters 40 and 41, two full years had been and gone and nothing had changed for Joseph. It's in these times of silence from God that we can start to doubt God's plan for our lives or even start questioning whether God really loves us or not.

These are the wilderness times in our lives, but they are so beneficial for not only character building but building a deep trust in God (even when God is silent) that we will love Him and serve Him in the place where He has us no matter what.

The verses in Isaiah 40: 29–31 should be one of our go-to verses in these times. In the New King James Version, it states:

> *He gives power to the weak, and to those who have no might He increases strength. Even the youths shall faint and grow weary, and the young man shall utterly fall, but those who wait on the Lord shall renew their strength; they shall mount up with wings like eagles, they shall run and not be weary, they shall walk and not faint.*

In these wilderness times, we can become weak and weary. However, the antidote in those times is to keep seeking the Lord and waiting on Him. Only God can get us through these times, so let's stop trying to do it in our own strength and just let Him get us through.

I love the words at the start of Genesis 41. The words are: 'Then it came to pass'. It's saying that it was time for God's plan to be fulfilled. It was time for God to move. We don't know what moves God to make His plans come to pass at a certain time. He sees the bigger picture, we don't. He sees from an eternal perspective, we don't. He sees the outcomes of His plan coming to pass at the right time, we don't. Sometimes it's hard to trust but let's continue until we're good at it.

Notice, however, it doesn't state in the verse, 'Then it came to pass that God moved in Joseph's life.' No, verse 1 states: "Then it came to pass... that Pharoah had a dream.'

Hang on, do you mean Joseph waited for God based on an ungodly person's dream? Yes, and the same can happen in our lives. Often God won't move until He knows our character is so developed in Him that we can impact the world around us and give Him all the glory. That is what the waiting is for, so that we can impact the world around us in a good way for God and His glory.

God always has eternity in mind and that means seeing as many of His creation turn to Him as possible. If this means we wait for God's timing for us, then we wait.

Pharaoh had a dream and who was the one whom God had raised up who was gifted in dream interpretation? Joseph. Last time, God had given Joseph dreams he was unwise with them and told everyone. This time, they were someone else's dreams. Often, we need to assist others with their dreams before ours are fulfilled.

Not only did Pharaoh have one dream, but he also had two and he had no idea what they meant. So he did what all good Pharaohs did—he called for all the wise magicians of Egypt and all the wise men (verse 8). But when he told them the dreams, they couldn't interpret them. Why? Because only a godly person can interpret a God dream.

I love what verses 9–13 state:

> *Then the chief butler spoke to Pharaoh, saying:*
> *"I remember my faults this day. When Pharaoh was angry with his servants, and put me in custody in the house of the captain of the guard, both me and the chief baker, we each had a dream in one night, he and I. Each of us dreamed according to the interpretation of his own dream. Now there was a young Hebrew man with us there, a servant of the captain of the guard. And we told him, and he interpreted our dreams for us; to each man he interpreted according to his own dream. And it came to pass, just as he interpreted for us, so it happened. He restored me to my office, and he hanged him.*

Our names and deeds are in places where our feet have not yet trod. God has people who know us in places we can't imagine. Here was Joseph in a prison and he knew someone in a palace because of circumstances only God could put together. This is the same for you and me. God is weaving our lives and connecting us with people who will have an impact on our future.

Pharaoh would probably have remembered this incident but had no idea of what had happened behind the scenes. He'd been involved at a distance but had been a part.

I like what the butler said about Joseph—that he was a servant of the captain of the guard and not a prisoner. Joseph would have seen himself as a prisoner. Sometimes, we can look at our lives in the waiting and see ourselves as less than we really are. We may see ourselves as just a mum or dad, but God sees evangelists raising up the next generation. We may see ourselves as a worker in a big city office, but God sees us as a potential leader learning leadership and mentoring skills to benefit the church. Think about your situation, turn it around and think about how God sees you.

This man's testimony paved the way for Joseph to be called to where God wanted him to be. Someone's testimony about you is going to do the same thing. Be ready but be humble and willing to obey God.

In verse 14, it states that Pharaoh called for Joseph. Pharaoh probably thought that he was a man who could help him. He didn't think of his nationality, education status or where he currently was but was more concerned with getting his needs met. God will minister through you and me in the same way to see the needs of others met.

What happened in verse 14 to Joseph is very similar to what God does with our lives when we give them to Him. Verse 14 states:

> *Then Pharaoh sent and called Joseph, and they brought him quickly out of the dungeon, and he shaved, changed his clothing, and came to Pharaoh.*

This is what we do when Jesus calls us—we change our clothing (who we represented; our old life) and put on new clothing (which is the righteousness of God) and we change our appearance from unkempt to become a son or daughter of the King.

A beautiful illustration of this is found in Zechariah 3:1–5. It states:

> *Then he showed me Joshua the high priest standing before the Angel of the Lord, and Satan standing at his right hand to oppose him. And the Lord said to Satan, "The Lord rebuke you, Satan! The Lord who has chosen Jerusalem rebuke you! Is this not a brand plucked from the fire?" Now Joshua was clothed with filthy garments, and was standing before the Angel. Then he answered and spoke to those who stood before Him, saying, "Take away the filthy garments from him." And to him He*

> *said," See, I have removed your iniquity from you, and I will clothe you with rich robes." And I said, "Let them put a clean turban on his head." So, they put a clean turban on his head, and they put the clothes on Him. And the Angel of the Lord stood by.*

This is a picture of us when we get saved. Jesus and Satan are standing there, waiting for our decision. Once we say 'yes to Jesus, Jesus rebukes Satan and calls us His son or daughter. Our filthy rags of sin, shame and guilt are removed from us and we are clothed with rich robes of righteousness. We are also given a clean turban, which is the authority we now carry.

I wonder what Joseph was thinking at this moment. Was he scared of what Pharaoh might do to him? Had he seen others be called to Pharaoh and never come back? This was a time for Joseph to trust in God. Joseph had held onto those dreams from God and maybe he thought they weren't going to be fulfilled. What was the urgency anyway? Did anyone actually tell Joseph why? The Bible doesn't tell us any of this and provides no answers. I wonder if the Bible is teaching us to totally trust in God in these moments.

In verse 15, Pharaoh reveals the reason for the haste. It was so Joseph could interpret his dream as nobody else could. Talk about being put on the spot! Isn't that sometimes what God does with us? He puts us on the spot to see if we have learnt the lessons He has been instilling in us. God puts situations in our path that are uncomfortable or even hard so

He can see where our trust in Him lies. Are we going to pass the test or do we need to go around the mountain again? This was a trust in God test for Joseph and a big one at that.

Verse 16 is the verse that sets Joseph's future in motion. It is all in how he answered Pharaoh. It states:

> *So, Joseph answered Pharaoh, saying, "It is not in me, God will give Pharaoh an answer of peace."*

It's in this moment that Joseph gives all the glory to God but also answers the heart of Pharaoh's issue—he has lost his peace because of this dream. If we trust in God, he will not only give us the answer to the issue at hand but also the remedy for the root cause of the issue.

Pharaoh told the dreams and Joseph interpreted them. Joseph's work was now done, or was it? He had been pulled out of prison to assist Pharaoh and now that the job was done, he would go back to prison. Right? Wrong! Joseph, with God's wisdom speaking through him, not only gives the interpretation of the dreams—seven years of plenty and seven years of famine—but also gives the solution as to how the country can survive the seven years of famine.

Often, in our haste to help others, we fall short of providing God's solution to the issue. We use our own experiences or what we read but not God's wisdom. Let's ask for it all the time in these circumstances as God can not only turn a person's life around but impact others and even a nation.

Joseph's solution (through God) for the issue is in verses 33–36. The verses state:

> *"Now therefore, let Pharaoh select a discerning and wise man, and set him over the land of Egypt. Let Pharaoh do this, and let him appoint officers over the land, to collect one-fifth of the produce of the land of Egypt in the seven plentiful years. And let them gather all the food of those good years that are coming, and store up grain under the authority of Pharaoh, and let them keep food in the cities. Then that food shall be as a reserve for the land for the seven years of famine which shall be in the land of Egypt, that the land may not perish during the famine."*

What happened next probably astounded Joseph more than appearing before Pharaoh did. Joseph was standing in the court of Pharaoh with all the magicians and the wise men of Egypt. Joseph's advice sounded good to Pharaoh and all his servants and in verse 38, Pharaoh makes this statement:

> *"Can we find such a one as this,
> a man in whom is the Spirit of God?"*

Pharaoh recognised that Joseph was being led by a higher power than even he had—the Spirit of God. When others see God in us, then not only will the wisdom coming out of our mouths astound them, they will see that we can be the answer to their issues (with God's help).

Pharaoh then addressed Joseph and in verses 39–41 made the following three statements:

- Inasmuch as God has shown you all this, there is no one as discerning and wise as you.
- You shall be over my house, and all my people shall be ruled according to your word; only in regard to the throne will I be greater than you.
- See, I have set you over all the land of Egypt.

Pharaoh recognised not only wisdom in Joseph's life but discernment. In the *Oxford Dictionary*, 'discernment' means the ability to judge well.

Discernment means we look at a situation, person or happening and we judge it rightly, not wrongly. This ability can only come from God as He alone knows the rights and wrongs of everything.

Joseph would now be over not only all the people but Pharaoh's house as well. What a big responsibility! He would rule over the prison and was no longer in it. When we come to God, we don't only come out of our prisons, we have the ability to rule over them because God is with us.

In verse 42, Pharaoh gives Joseph his signet ring (authority), puts him in new clothes (righteousness) and puts a gold chain around his neck (value).

When we come to Jesus and make Him our Saviour and Lord, He also gives us these three things:

1. Authority—Matthew 28:18–20

   Jesus said (after He had been to the cross and risen again) that all authority had now been given to Him on earth and in heaven and then He told us to go. In essence, Jesus transferred the authority to us so we could do the tasks He stated next:

   - Make disciples of all nations
   - Baptise those disciples in the name of the Father, the Son and the Holy Spirit
   - Teach those disciples to observe all Jesus' commandments

   In Mark 16:17–18, it further commands us to:

   - Cast out demons
   - Speak with new tongues
   - Lay hands on the sick and they will recover
   - Nothing harmful will touch us e.g. serpents and deadly drinks

   When we are walking in the authority of Jesus, we can do what He did if we have faith and believe we can.

2. Righteousness—2 Corinthians 5:21

   This verse tells us that because Jesus was made sin for us on the cross, we can now become the righteousness of God in Jesus.

   Righteousness in this verse means that God declares us righteous in the sense of acquitting us from our sin (like in a court of law) and our reward is that God imparts righteousness to us, which is the quality of being right. This enables us to walk boldly into the throne room of God to pray because without righteousness, this would not be possible. Sin cannot enter into the presence of God.

3. Value—sons and daughters of God—Galatians 4:4–7

   We now have value as sons and daughters of God. When Jesus did what He did on the cross and rose again, we now have the right to say 'yes' to God and be adopted into His family. This means we are no longer slaves to sin but sons and daughters of God and heirs to all God has. This means that deliverance is ours, healing is ours, love is ours, the fruit of the spirit is ours, protection is ours and provision is ours. What a great way to live!

   However, we need to learn to walk in all three and not be intimidated by Satan when he tells us we are not worthy. We are worthy because of Jesus. This is a process and that's why God says that He's changing us from glory to glory—from one level to the next—so that we can become more like Jesus.

This is the journey from the prison to the palace, but it doesn't end there. There are still things and people in Joseph's past that need to be dealt with and it's the same in our lives.

The next chapters of this book will talk about the things that needed to be healed in Joseph's life.

Let's pray:

*God, we are so grateful to you that just like Joseph was
brought from the prison to the palace in a moment,
we can be brought from our prison to Jesus in a moment
when we say 'yes'. We are so thankful, God,
that You have made a way for us to be free and
to live our lives daily being changed to be
more like Jesus. Thank you! Amen.*

# CHAPTER 10

# **FORGIVENESS**

Forgiveness is a word that sometimes we use as a religious cliché. Just forgive them, it will be okay, and we're expected to get through the journey of forgiveness in less than a minute. However, I believe, as I have looked and meditated on the story of Joseph, that forgiveness is more of a wrestle in our lives. We know what to do but the hurt and betrayal of a situation can sometimes seem impossible to navigate.

Forgiveness also seems to be a concept where just saying the word lets the other person walk away with no consequences so inside, we wrestle with this concept.

We know that Jesus forgave us of our sins and that we're meant to forgive others, but whilst we accept what Jesus did for us, the concept of offering the same thing to others seems hard.

Forgiveness has two meanings in the Greek, which are:

1. *Charidzomia* comes from the word *'charis'*, which means grace. Forgiveness can mean we offer grace (the unmerited favour of God) to the other person. It means cancelling their debt.
2. *Alphiemi*, which means 'loose' or 'let go'. It means never to bring up again.

The first word centres around the concept of forgiving a person so they don't owe us anything. This is much like a loan or a mortgage is cancelled. They are free to continue their lives and so are we.

The second word centres around the concept of letting it go and never bringing it up again. Although we remember how that person has wronged us, the hurt of it has no hold over our lives, and therefore, we never speak of it again.

Both of the meanings can involve a wrestle as we say we forgive someone and then, with God's help, forget the hurt they caused, setting them free. The word 'free' doesn't mean that God doesn't make them account for their wrongdoing, it means that we are no longer shackled to them by unforgiveness. Unforgiveness shackles or ties us to the other person. It's like we're dragging them with us wherever we go.

As we consider Joseph's story, let's remember that forgiving someone can be a wrestle. We can walk two steps forward and one step back until the process of forgiveness is completed.

Forgiveness is also an act of faith. It's a deliberate action on our part that doesn't involve feelings. If we waited to feel good before we forgave, it would never happen. Jesus was dying on a cross when He forgave those around Him.

Joseph was now second in charge in Egypt. He was married with two sons. The seven plentiful years had begun, and the ground brought forth abundantly (Genesis 41:47).

Joseph gathered 20% of all the grain and stored it up for those seven years of famine. In verse 49, the Bible states that Joseph stopped counting the grain as it was immeasurable. Surely, they would have enough.

In the plentiful years in our lives, we need to make provision for those lean times. I'm not talking about monetary things but spiritual things. In those plentiful times, don't forget to read the Bible, pray and attend church because the day of famine could be just around the corner when you desperately need what you stored in your heart during that plentiful season.

Jesus modelled this for us beautifully. He knew that the cross was coming so He did everything He could to show us how to live our lives God's way whilst He could. He healed the sick, raised the dead, provided twice for a huge number of people, taught the disciples the right way of living and generally gave people all He could. This was so that after the cross and the resurrection, the disciples could continue the work of Jesus on the earth. He modelled living a plentiful life before the famine came.

Jesus rose from the dead and then communicated more with His disciples for 40 days. Then Jesus was taken up (Acts 1:9). What happened to those disciples? Verse 14 of Acts 1 tells us:

> *These all continued with one accord in prayer and supplications...*

Why? Because in those years of plenty with Jesus, they'd learnt what to do.

In those years of plenty in our lives, learn all about Jesus and His ways and then when those storms come—and they will—you will know what to do—continue.

In verse 53 of Genesis 41, it states that the years of plenty ended. Then came the seven years of famine. It's in those times of famine that it can feel like the enemy is attacking us harder. But famine does not mean defeat, it means lack. 'Lack' does not mean defeat, it means that something is missing from our lives e.g. a bad diagnosis, a job loss, a child deciding not to follow Jesus, a spouse leaving us behind, a move to another city, a church move, a change of job, etc. Lack can mean many things and for each of us at different times in our lives, it will take on a different meaning, depending on our circumstances.

Verse 55 is interesting to me as the people went to their leader to satisfy their lack but the leader sent them to Joseph. Often our leaders may not be able to assist in our time of lack, but they can point you to someone who can. All of us are in the body of Christ, which means we each have a part to play, even our leaders. They may be our pastors and are part of the arm in the body of Christ, but it doesn't mean they know how to perform the leg's role. The leg's role might be just what we need to help us through our lack. You need wisdom for your situation, not familiarity or leadership time.

Verse 57 is where everything changes for Joseph and his family. The verse states:

> *So, all countries came to Joseph in Egypt to buy grain, because the famine was severe in all lands.*

This verse changes everything because if all countries were now coming, the chances of Joseph's family coming were high. It's easy to forget about how people have treated you if you have made a new life for yourself and are far away. But when circumstances change, you may be about to be confronted by something or someone where healing needs to take place.

Chapter 42 of Genesis is titled in my Bible 'Joseph's Brothers Go to Egypt'. If you didn't know the story, this title might seem a little odd. But when you do, you will know that this story has the potential to heal or destroy people's lives.

Jacob and his sons had no idea of the life that Joseph now lived in Egypt. If his brothers thought about him at all, it was possibly to consider that Joseph was no longer alive because nobody could survive a slave trader. Joseph was the last person they thought they would ever see again, let alone be the person that they needed to buy grain from.

So off they went willingly. Verse 8 of chapter 42 is interesting, and it states:

> *So, Joseph recognised his brothers,*
> *but they did not recognise him.*

Joseph wasn't the same person who had left home around 20 years earlier. He was not a slave but the governor of a foreign land. He looked different, spoke differently and was dressed differently. His brothers also weren't expecting to see him.

For Joseph it was different. Once others from different lands started coming to Egypt to buy grain, he probably wondered if and when they would come. He was probably expecting them and maybe was looking out for them.

On their first encounter, Joseph treated them harshly and questioned them about everything. This was probably not normal and the people serving with him probably wondered about his behaviour. Joseph was hungry for knowledge about his father and brother. He'd kept them hidden for a long time and had probably suppressed his memory of them, but he couldn't do that anymore. It was time to deal with the unforgiveness in all parties.

Just a note on unforgiveness. It's generally not on its own in our lives. It generally couples with bitterness, hardness of heart, walls, jealousy, insecurity and a host of other things. Once it's broken off our lives, other things will be broken too.

The forgiveness journey also involves both parties, whether they want to acknowledge it or not. Jesus told us to forgive our enemies. Our enemies are anyone who we don't love unconditionally as God loves them.

Sometimes we feel that God is asking us to forgive and the other party gets off lightly. But that is never the case. The same command that applies to us will apply to them when they give their hearts to Jesus, or they will go to the grave with the consequences of unforgiveness still ravaging their hearts.

The reason Jesus told us to forgive was so that we could be free. The other person's freedom is between them and God. However, when we offer forgiveness, which we can, it often frees the other person as well, especially if they belong to Jesus.

Obedience to God is always better than harbouring unforgiveness towards others.

Unforgiveness caused Joseph to put all his brothers in prison for three days according to Genesis 42:17. Was this revenge for his prison sentence or did he need time to deal with seeing his brothers, so he kept them close? I am not sure but after three days, in verses 18–20, Joseph stated:

> *"Do this and live, for I fear God. If you are honest men, let one of your brothers be confined to your prison house, but you, go and carry grain for the families of*

> *your houses. And bring your youngest brother to me, so your words will be verified, and you shall not die."*

In those three days of the brothers' confinement in prison, God must have spoken to Joseph about forgiving his brothers. Therefore, he let most of them go back to their families.

But because Joseph didn't reveal himself to his brothers, the story is not complete. One of his brothers was still in prison and Joseph may have been tormented by this fact (I wonder if he ever visited him). He was probably hoping that his brothers would return to Egypt quickly the second time, bringing their brother Benjamin with them.

Sometimes we are the same. We forgive enough to allow ourselves to be appeased but not totally restored. Joseph could never be totally restored to his family until he revealed his identity.

When we keep part of ourselves back from forgiving others because we want justice or we keep part of ourselves back from God when telling Him we are sorry, we can't be totally restored. Forgiveness requires our whole selves.

Generally, it's our soul (our emotions and thoughts about the situation) that is the last to heal. If you have sustained physical injuries, they will heal and generally, your relationship with God will be sound, but your soul will still be a mess. This is the hardest area to recover because it's our most vulnerable area and the area we feel the most.

King Saul and David's relationship in the end was similar. King Saul could never forgive David, and ultimately God, for anointing David king whilst Saul was still alive. This meant the kingship would not pass down to his sons. This relationship could therefore, never be totally restored.

Just a note of warning. We can forgive people who have abused and hurt us badly and we should, but the relationship may never be restored fully. This is where grace comes in. We need the power of God to work in our hearts in these situations to restore us fully. We don't want to relive those moments or that hurt ever again, and it requires the Holy Spirit's intervention. Full restoration requires that the element of trust is restored, which may not ever happen.

Let's look at the last physical encounter between King Saul and David to get some context. It is found in 1 Samuel 26. The Ziphites told Saul that David was hiding in the hill of Hachillah so Saul went down there with 3000 Israelite soldiers to war against David and his few hundred men. Seems like an easy battle, but it wasn't as it wasn't in God. Just because we have an army coming against us doesn't mean they will defeat us.

David found out that Saul had come once again to hunt him down and sent out spies to confirm. Once he had confirmed this, he decided to go down into Saul's camp in the night with one of his men.

Abishai told David to kill Saul, but David wouldn't as he knew not to touch the king and leader that God had appointed over him. God wouldn't have been pleased with David if he'd done this, even though Saul was in the wrong. The role that

Saul held was greater than Saul's sin. Read that again! It's not up to us to take vengeance for ourselves if someone has wronged us. Our job is to forgive and let God deal with them. Reaping will come to them if we don't take matters into our own hands.

So what did David do? He had to prove to King Saul once again that he was not his enemy. He took the water jug and the king's spear and went to the top of the hill, which was a great distance away. It's never wise to get too close to those who make themselves our enemies when we confront them.

David stood on top of that hill and shouted to Abner, the commander of Saul's army. He basically stated, 'Why have you not protected your master? We came into the camp and took the water jug and the spear whilst you were all sleeping (God put them in a deep sleep). You did a bad job! I could have killed all of you!'

In verse 17, Saul calls David his son, which he is as he was also his son-in-law, but these words denote relationship and not enmity. Be aware of those who use flattering words and seek to restore the relationship with flattering words and not true forgiveness.

In verse 21, Saul states, 'I have sinned.' But were Saul's words true or were they in-the-moment words? Saul knew David could have killed him so were his words because David spared his life or was it real forgiveness? Based on Saul's past, we can only assume it was partial forgiveness and not a total restoration.

David knew it too because in chapter 27, he went and lived in Philistine country instead of in Israel. He was safer in real enemy territory than his own nation.

Verse 4 of that chapter confirms the partial forgiveness. It states: 'And it was told Saul that David had fled to Gath; so, he sought him no more.'

The relationship between King Saul and David was never restored because of Saul's insecurities in relation to his own leadership. If David had remained with Saul, what amazing feats he might have done under King Saul's leadership and then David might have been the king of peace and built God's temple.

Let's quickly have a look at the life of Jesus. Jesus forgave everyone at the cross and He spoke these words, 'Father, forgive them for they know not what they are doing.'

Jesus forgave everyone but His relationship with everyone was not restored. He opened the door for people to accept His forgiveness, but He doesn't make people have a restored relationship with Him. Jesus doesn't forgive unconditionally. He loves unconditionally but if we don't accept His forgiveness, there are consequences (not for Him but for us).

The Pharisees may never have restored their relationship with Him, but that was their choice. Sometimes in our own lives, once we forgive someone, the relationship may never be restored but we need to ensure our hearts are not bitter towards them. Just remember, Jesus forgave Judas at the cross. It's just that Judas couldn't forgive himself.

Sometimes, that is the hardest thing—to forgive ourselves. But once we come to Jesus and He has forgiven us, we should never not be able to forgive ourselves. If not, we make ourselves higher than Jesus, which isn't right. If Jesus forgives us, we should forgive us.

Your future depends on total forgiveness and not partial forgiveness.

Let's pray at the close of this chapter before we look at the story of total forgiveness and how it's possible with the restoration of relationship.

> *Father, we thank you that you have provided us with the mechanism of forgiveness so that we can live free and not be in bondage to another person anymore. Where we have partially forgiven someone, please give us the wisdom to be able to either restore the relationship, if possible, or have total peace in our hearts regarding those previous events and circumstances. Thank you for your Holy Spirit and the gift of grace. Amen.*

CHAPTER 11

# RESTORATION

When we left the last chapter, we were talking about partial forgiveness. This may be all that can happen in certain circumstances such as abuse, neglect, etc. Total forgiveness can only come with the restoration of relationship.

I want to take a deeper dive into forgiveness here. I believe that the forgiveness journey in our life can oftentimes be a wrestle. Sometimes forgiveness will be instant and other times it will be a journey we go on.

For example, two children are playing in a sand pit. One hits the other one and makes them cry. The adults come along and tell the child who hit the other to say sorry, which they do. A minute later, both children are happily playing again.

We want this to be our forgiveness story too and often it is, but sometimes deep hurts can make forgiving others become more like a journey. God meets us each step of the way.

The first step we talked about in chapter 10. We need to forgive others as God has forgiven us. This is the action of saying it and believing it but often things that can restore relationships take a lot longer, if they happen at all.

The next steps are revealing who you now are and the restoration of the relationship. In some circumstances, these things may be impossible because it may be dangerous for you to speak to the other person about who you now are and what God has done in your life and the restoration of that relationship. Sometimes you might just want to write a letter and send it or put it in the bin. This may be closure for you.

Don't ever put yourself in a dangerous situation. Just leave it with God.

We left Joseph's story with only partial forgiveness taking place. He let most of his brothers go back to Canaan with food for their families but kept one brother locked up in prison. He gave them their money back, which they found in their sacks later that first night after leaving Egypt.

Joseph seemed to be on his journey of forgiving his brothers but as we will see through the next part of the story, he had to wrestle through his emotions and the reconciliation.

The brothers were perplexed about the whole situation. They were probably thinking that this type of situation didn't appear to be happening to anyone else in the line for food. So why them? When they found the money, they were more afraid.

Did fear prevent them from returning or did lack of food cause them to go back again? What would they have been thinking?

When they returned to their father, they told him the whole story and he was really upset. He had lost Joseph and now another one of his sons was in prison in a foreign land. His heart couldn't take losing Benjamin as well. So their return to Egypt was delayed.

Finally, Genesis 43:1 states that the famine was severe in the land and in verse 2, the family had eaten all the grain. It was time to make the decision to return to Egypt to buy more food.

Jacob told his sons to go back but there now came a wrestling. Sometimes in our journey of forgiveness, there is a wrestling that occurs that we're not aware of at the time.

Jacob's sons couldn't go back to Egypt without Benjamin and therefore, Jacob had to make a choice. He could potentially lose another son but save his whole family. This time though, Jacob sent a present to the man to appease him (verse 11). Where they got the best fruits of the land and the rest of the goods in a famine is probably a miracle in itself.

Let's stop and take note of what has happened in the story.

> Jacob—a man who had now lost two sons out of 12 but knew he needed to sacrifice a third to save his family.

> The brothers—this time going back to Egypt was a frightening journey, as they didn't know what was going to transpire.
>
> Benjamin—going with the brothers to stand before this man in Egypt, not knowing who he was.
>
> Simeon—still in prison and hoping his family wasn't going to forget about him.
>
> Joseph—looking out each day wondering when, not if, his brothers would return.

Our journey to restoration and forgiveness can be a lot like this. It can be frightening, it can cause doubts, we can wonder whether God is still with us and most importantly, we know that in most cases, restoration and forgiveness can involve sacrifice.

In verse 15, the brothers stand before Joseph, probably nervous and apprehensive. But what the man did next was totally unexpected—he invited them to dinner. They became more afraid and sought to give the money back to the steward of Joseph's house (who was Egyptian).

What this steward said in verse 23 is astonishing:

> *"Peace be with you, do not be afraid.*
> *Your God and the God of your father has given you*
> *treasure in your sacks; I had your money."*

Notice that the steward had no idea who these men were and their relationship to Joseph. It was like God was speaking through him to reassure them.

God will always do this with us. He walks through our forgiveness journey with us. He will constantly be whispering to us, 'Don't be afraid, I am with you.'

Simeon was also released back to them, which would have been a joyous time for all the brothers.

Joseph came in and ate dinner with them but went out weeping as his heart yearned for his brother. Have you ever felt like that in a broken relationship, where your heart yearns to be reunited and restored? Sometimes it's possible but sometimes it's not, so we need to go to God and allow Him to heal those broken bits of our hearts.

After dinner, the steward filled the men's sacks with food and their money, and he was instructed by Joseph to put his silver cup in Benjamin's sack. Then he sent them on their way the next day. Why would Joseph do this? Was his heart not ready to forgive his brothers? Did he want them near for a moment but not for a lifetime? What was he thinking?

Unforgiveness left festering in our hearts for a long time can make our hearts bitter and sick. It can also be buried until we are confronted with the situation or person again. It's in these moments that the wrestle of forgiveness is taking place.

I believe that Joseph was wrestling with unforgiveness. His brothers had wanted to kill him but instead had thrown him into a pit and sold him. Were the thoughts consuming Joseph greater than the dreams of his family bowing down to him that God had promised a long time ago?

Was Joseph scared of his brothers or was he scared of what he was capable of doing to them? After all, he was second in charge in Egypt. Does the power or position placed around our lives give us the right to not forgive?

The brothers were just out of the city limits when Joseph sent the steward after them to retrieve his silver cup. Joseph knew if the brothers found it first they would come back with it or try to hide it and continue on their journey.

The brothers were perplexed when the steward came after them, stopped them and accused them of stealing. They even told the steward that the one who had stolen the cup should die not realising it was a set-up. They were probably watched the whole time they were in Joseph's house and wouldn't have had a chance to steal anything.

The cup was found in Benjamin's sack and again the brothers packed up, went into Egypt and bowed in front of Joseph. This time they begged for their brother as their father couldn't handle the burden of losing another son.

Joseph was still wrestling with unforgiveness towards his brothers as he wanted Benjamin to stay with him but the others to go. The only thing that broke Joseph was the burden his father would go through if both sons of his wife Rachel, were lost to him.

Finally, in chapter 45:1, Joseph reveals himself to his brothers. There was a time of disbelief and then joy. Verse 5 sums it all up. It states:

> *But now, do not therefore be grieved or angry with yourselves because you sold me here; for God sent me before you to preserve life.*

Did this mean the restoration of the relationship was complete with all the brothers? Yes, I think from Joseph's perspective, all was forgiven. Not so his brothers, which we will touch on further down.

Verses 14 and 15 of chapter 45 tell us this:

> *Then he fell on his brother Benjamin's neck and wept, and Benjamin wept on his neck. Moreover, he kissed all his brothers and wept over them, and after that his brothers talked with him.*

Healing and forgiveness happen in the power of touch. A hug tells us that all is now right with our world. It's a place of safety and security. You don't hug just anyone and certainly not someone for whom you feel unforgiveness.

However, we can see some keys here that Joseph used to bring closure for him. They are:

1. He revealed himself. He was no longer in hiding but came out so that the relationship could be restored.
2. He named their sin. He said that he was their brother, who they'd sold into Egypt.
3. He looked at the higher purpose. 'It was God who sent me here through your actions, but it was to fulfil a greater purpose for others.'
4. He advised them of his new identity. He was a father to Pharaoh and lord of all his house and a ruler throughout all the land of Egypt.
5. He knew other relationships needed to be restored. He advised them to hurry and get his father and bring him down to see him.
6. He provided a place for them to be near him. 'You shall dwell in the land of Goshen.'

Jacob's bitter and hard heart revived when he heard that Joseph was still alive (verse 27).

Why did I mention before that forgiveness had not happened fully to his brothers? Let's have a look at the story in chapter 50:15–21.

It states in part:

> *When Joseph's brothers saw that their father was dead, they said, "Perhaps Joseph will hate us, and may actually repay us for all the evil which we did to him." So, they sent messengers to Joseph saying, "Before your father died, he commanded, saying, 'Thus you shall say to Joseph: "I beg you, please forgive the trespass of your brothers and their sin; for they did evil to you." 'Now, please, forgive the trespass of the servants of the God of your father." And Joseph wept when they spoke to him. Then his brothers also went and fell down before his face, and they said, "Behold, we are your servants."*
>
> *Joseph said to them, "Do not be afraid, for am I in the place of God? But as for you, you meant evil against me; but God meant it for good, in order to bring it about as it is this day, to save many people alive. Now therefore, do not be afraid; I will provide for you and your little ones". And he comforted them and spoke kindly to them.*

Joseph's brothers still had not dealt totally with the forgiveness offered to them by him. They had harboured it in their hearts for many years after Joseph had first forgiven them. This probably led to a fractured relationship with Joseph. On the surface, everything probably looked okay, but not inside.

This is why it's important to rely on the Holy Spirit and His wisdom. Not only does the Holy Spirit help us to forgive but He can also reveal any underlying things that need to be dealt with.

Sometimes our unforgiveness towards a person can affect others and also needs to be dealt with in their lives. This is especially the case when you have an influence on the person e.g. a parent, child or best friend.

Forgiveness of others can break bondage over not only our lives and the perpetrator's life but also over others who are affected. In our story, Jacob would have been a person who'd been affected by what had transpired.

The last two chapters have only touched on forgiveness and restoration of relationships. If you need further guidance with this, please seek your pastor's or a trusted friend's or counsellor's input. It's time for you to get free. Let's pray:

> *Father, thank you that as You forgive us, we forgive others. It's a flow-on effect that can only be stopped by us carrying unforgiveness. Please help us to forgive those who have wronged us and please give us guidance and direction if any relationships need to be restored. We thank you for Your grace and mercy towards us. In Jesus' name, amen.*

CHAPTER 12

# PEACE

Although the cycle of unforgiveness and restoration goes on in a circle in our lives, we can come to the stage where peace can rule.

What is peace? Peace for most of us means the absence of conflict but I'm not sure that's a good definition as conflicts will always find us, but we need to learn to live in peace.

One of the words for peace in the Old Testament is shalom. I really like this word because it encompasses so much. It means completeness, wholeness, peace, health, welfare, safety, soundness, tranquility, prosperity, perfection, fullness, rest and harmony. Re-read those words and let it settle within you that this is all yours in Jesus.

Nowhere in that list of words does hate, anger, war, rudeness, selfishness, self-centredness or meanness enter in. That first list sounds like the perfect world, which was in Eden.

Genesis 1 is our only reference to a perfect world but a world more perfect is coming, one where Satan and therefore sin cannot enter at all. This is heaven.

In the Garden of Eden, there was everything we needed to live an amazing life. There were trees, sun, light, night, oceans, animals and other people. There was food that was nourishment to our bodies and not harmful to us. Most of all, there was a pure relationship with God. This is our ideal world, where peace rules.

But there was one thing in the Garden of Eden that goes with peace and that is rest. In Genesis 2:2–3, it states that God ended his work and He rested on the seventh day. He then blessed this day and sanctified it.

Peace and rest go hand in hand, but these words don't mean laziness. In verse 15 of Genesis 2, God put the man in the garden to tend and keep it. Each of us has a calling from God on our lives that we need to fulfil, and it involves tending to the calling and keeping it by working.

Joseph had revealed himself to his brothers and had been reconciled to his father. He then moved his family from Canaan to Egypt and settled them in the land of Goshen, where the brothers could continue to do the work that they were best at—tending livestock.

In Genesis 47:11–12, it states:

> *And Joseph situated his father and his brothers,*
> *and gave them a possession in the land of Egypt,*

> *in the best of the land, in the land of Rameses,*
> *as Pharaoh had commanded. Then Joseph provided his*
> *father, his brothers, and all his father's household with*
> *bread, according to the number in their families.*

Joseph's brothers, dad and their families now had peace and rest. They no longer had to travel a long distance to get their food during the famine. They no longer had to worry and be anxious about how to feed their families. They had total peace and therefore, total rest, as Joseph took care of them.

What did Joseph do after he had settled his family? He went back to dealing with the Egyptians and others regarding the next five years of famine. His work didn't stop because his family had peace and rest. No, he had a calling to undertake but he probably performed that calling with greater purpose and more peace over his own life.

He would have been more content knowing his dad and brother Benjamin were safe, as well as the rest of his brothers.

Joseph would have been more secure in knowing that God was with him and he probably no longer felt rejected by his family and therefore, insecurity was no longer an issue. Joseph knew he was deeply loved by people for who he really was and that probably made all the difference in his life.

Sometimes when we have fractured family relationships with the people who really know us, we can put on a façade for those who don't. It's only when we know that first we are deeply loved by God, then deeply loved by those we care about, that our lives can be more peaceful and restful.

For me, anxiety rears its ugly head when I don't remember that God loves me and God is protecting me. When situations come around my life and I feel alone, that is when the enemy attacks and makes me feel unloved.

All of us need community around us in order to feel totally at peace and totally at rest.

I want to have a look at two psalms before we look at the life of Jesus in relation to peace and rest. Both of these psalms are well known but I think it's good for us to review them in light of peace and rest.

The first is Psalm 23 and it states:

- The Lord is my shepherd; I shall not want.
- He makes me lie down in green pastures; He leads me beside the still waters.
- He restores my soul; He leads me in the paths of righteousness for His name's sake.
- Yea, though I walk through the valley of the shadow of death, I will fear no evil; for You are with me; Your rod and Your staff, they comfort me.
- You prepare a table before me in the presence of my enemies; You anoint my head with oil; My cup runs over.
- Surely goodness and mercy shall follow me all the days of my life; and I will dwell in the house of the Lord forever.

There are six sections in this psalm that I just want to have a look at that will help us live in peace and rest.

The first is that God is my shepherd and because of that, I want for nothing. Let's think about what a shepherd does. They:

- Protect
- Feed
- Find water
- Apply healing salve
- Find shelter in the storms
- Ward off enemies
- Feed the lambs
- Touch the sheep

Can you see from this what God does for us? We can have rest because God does all of the above for you and me. We just forget sometimes in those stormy moments of life. We can see from the above list that the sheep don't want for anything unless they stray. If they keep close to the shepherd, they know that the shepherd will supply everything they need. What a beautiful picture of God's love for us!

The second is that God makes us lie down in green pastures and leads us beside still waters. This speaks of rest to me. When we lie down in the grass, we relax because the grass is not brown and prickly but green and lush.

I am writing this from the coast, and we are staying in a unit on the calm side of a passage that leads out to the sea. Every time I look at the water or walk beside it, a calmness comes to my soul. I wonder what it is about calm water that can lead to peace and rest. Is it because the water gently laps into the shore, and it's constant and at peace? The water is not roaring like the waves do at the surf beach, but they gently come in. When we perceive calm, do we become calm?

God doesn't give me a choice about whether to lie down in green grass. He makes me. Why does He do that? Because He knows that rest is what I require if I am to keep going on my journey for Him. God rested and so should we. We need to incorporate a weekly Sabbath day into our lives to enable ourselves to be at peace and rest and to shut out the busyness and rush of the world we live in. It's time to rest and be at peace.

The third thing is that God not only restores my soul, but He leads me in the paths of righteousness. 'Paths' is plural, which means there is more than one path to righteousness. Righteousness means being right with God. There are many facets of Who God is and each one is a path that we must undertake in order to find the fullness of Who God is.

As we walk through those paths of righteousness, our soul is restored. For example, as we walk the path of learning patience because God is patient, then our soul is restored in this area. The same goes for all the fruit of the spirit found in Galatians 5.

However, we also need to walk those paths of being right with God in our spiritual disciplines like reading the Bible, praying, worship, praise, church attendance, etc. These all help to reveal the fullness of God to us. Just a note, we will never know God fully until we get to heaven and even then, we will still learn more.

We also need to walk the paths of calling—knowing exactly what God created us to do before the foundation of the world. There are also the gifts of the Holy Spirit that we may need to learn to walk in.

These are just some of the paths God will lead us to walk and it's all for Him. Don't be scared of these paths; embrace them. It's where you will find rest and peace.

The fourth thing is that even though we are promised peace and rest, sometimes it can look the opposite in our lives. This is where verse 4 comes in. Even though we walk through what we call hard times—the Bible calls it the valley of the shadow of death—we walk through it. It's not a camping spot where we feel that we can sit and think woe is me and tell everyone our troubles. No, it's a time to trust God more and keep walking through.

I love how the verse states that we will fear no evil and that comes first. It means that fear will come but we need to remember the next part—that God is with us. God's rod and staff will comfort us. What does this mean? A rod is there to direct me back onto the right path if I stray. It can feel like punishment, but it's really discipline that keeps us on the right track. It's the same with our children—we discipline them to get them back to the right way of living or to keep them out of harm's way, like a hot stove.

The staff is there to pick us up and bring us back; it's a compassion and care tool. When we fall down a hole, the staff is there to retrieve us and put us back. The rod guides and the staff retrieves. This is a beautiful picture of our daily walk with God and leads to peace and rest.

The fifth thing is that God prepares for us a table in the presence of our enemies. God gives us provision for whatever we need. A table is a place of sustenance as well as provision. In the times in our lives when the enemy is attacking us the hardest, as his tactics are easily seen, God provides us what we need to defeat the enemy as a table of provision.

The sustenance God provides us with is His Word, prayer, praise, worship, meditating on Him, thinking good thoughts, confession of sins, confessing the Word over our lives that pertains to the situation, the fruit of the Spirit and so much more. But it is up to us to take of that provision to find peace and rest.

God also anoints us with oil. This declares that we are His priests in the Kingdom of God. We have the right to go into the throne room of grace and ask for what we need. It's a symbol of belonging and the authority that God has placed over our lives. When we know our position in the Kingdom of God, this brings peace and rest.

The sixth thing is our response to the other five things above. We can declare that goodness and mercy will follow us and be our constant companions. We can live in the goodness of all God has for us and that God's mercy will be there for us when we need it. This is not a short-term thing but for all the days of our lives.

The best part of all this is that we will dwell in the house of God forever. If we keep God close in our lives, then we will dwell with him forever, in His spiritual presence whilst we are on earth and then in His full presence once we get to heaven. What a glorious day that will be! Rest and peace will be our constant companions.

Psalm 91 is the other psalm that I love that provides the assurance of rest and peace. I am not going to go through it in detail. I encourage you to read it, think on it and memorise it as the words in this psalm are going to sustain us through all the challenges of the world we currently live in and will bring us rest and peace.

In my Bible, it is titled 'Safety of Abiding in the Presence of God'. Just reading that title brings rest and peace as we know we will be safe if we continue to abide in the presence of God.

Let's look at a couple of key points. The first one is that this psalm only applies to those who fit into verse 1a. We need to be those who dwell in the secret place of God. Are you in the secret place with God? What is a secret place?

I remember when I was a child and we had secret places where we met with our friends and we believed our parents or little brothers and sisters couldn't find us. It was a place where we hid away for a time to spend time and share secrets with those we wanted to. It's the same with our relationship with God. We need to find that place where we can hide away from others and just be in the presence of God so we can share our secrets with Him and He can share His secrets with us. It's in this place where we can feel hidden and protected.

This secret place can be a physical place, but it's hard to remain there all day. We need to make sure that God resides within us and that we are aware of His presence with us all day every day. This is the secret place—a place we can go to continually to meet with God.

Verse 2 of this psalm talks about our response to being in the secret place. It states:

> *I will say of the Lord, "He is my refuge and my fortress;*
> *My God in Him I will trust."*

To dwell in that secret place and find safety there, our response must always be to trust in God. He is the all-present one and the all-knowing one and only He has the capacity to keep us safe and protected, but only when we abide in Him.

Notice that our response comes first before it tells us everything that God will do for us. Our place and our response need to come first always. A verse that this is very clear on is found in James 4:8a, which states:

*Draw near to God and He will draw near to you.*

Jesus did everything necessary on the cross for our salvation and our place in the Kingdom of God. But we must accept this by faith. We must draw near first so God knows we are serious about pursuing Him.

Once God knows we are serious about pursuing him and that we have positioned ourselves in the place of abiding and put our trust in Him, then He can shower us with all good things. In Psalm 91, starting at verse 3, those good things are:

- Deliver us from traps and pestilences
- Cover us with his feathers under his wings
- God's truth will be our shield of faith
- We shall not fear the circumstances around us
- We will be safe in God
- No evil or plague can touch us
- We will have angels caring for us
- God will answer us when we call
- God will give us a long life and will continually show us what life looks like with Him

These are all great promises when it comes to our peace and rest but remember to receive them, we must position ourselves in God and trust Him.

Let's glimpse into the life of Jesus in relation to rest and peace. Being in rest and peace doesn't mean lying around all day in bed or on the couch watching shows. It means having peace and rest around our lives and factored into our lives in the midst of the busyness of the day.

One of the stories in Jesus' life perfectly shows both peace and rest. It's found in a few of the gospels, but I am going to look at the account in Luke 8:22–25. It's the story of the wind and waves obeying Jesus. That's a miracle in itself, but I want to have a look at this story in the context of peace and rest.

Verse 22 has a very important statement that we often miss. Jesus got into the boat with his disciples and made this statement:

*"Let us cross over to the other side of the lake."*

Now as far as Jesus was concerned, He had given a command, and it was to be carried out. He spoke it out loud so everyone; even Satan could hear.

Then, in verse 23, Jesus fell asleep. He had given a command to cross over to the other side of the lake, which He knew would take a while. As He wasn't a seasoned fisherman like some of His disciples, He decided to get some rest and He fell asleep. He meant to stay that way until they reached the other side. But who knows? In the middle of our strategic rest time, something might come up that we didn't expect.

It's the same with our children. You tell them that Mummy is going to take a rest for a while, and it seems bedlam then occurs. The kids fight, they come in every couple of minutes as they want a snack or to show you something and very soon, that strategic rest time is over.

This is what happened to Jesus, although it was His disciples coming to wake Him.

A big windstorm rose and was flooding the boat. It must have been some storm as some of these disciples were fishermen and would have seen and navigated through storms before or did they forget their previous training? I'm not sure.

They woke Jesus up to tell Him of this windstorm. Did Jesus shout and have a fit because they woke Him? No, He just dealt with the storm by rebuking it until it was calm. Then He asked the disciples, 'Where is your faith?'

In the midst of the strategic rest time for Jesus, a storm arose. This can happen when we make time for rest. Our response should not be to get upset at the disruption but to rebuke the spirit behind it and go back to rest. Oftentimes, we get upset because we don't recognise what is trying to derail us.

As we go throughout our day, we can walk in this rest too, aware that the enemy is out there seeking to get us off course from rest and peace in our lives.

I have struggled with this and will make sure in my own life that I'm constantly looking out for triggers to make me feel restless and in turmoil. For me, it's often when I am tired and haven't taken the time, when able, to physically sleep.

In relation to Jesus and peace, if you read all four gospels you will see that Jesus was never in a hurry but just went around doing good according to what His Father's instructions were to Him.

The best story that shows this peace is the story around the woman with the issue of blood and Jairus' daughter. We don't often see two miracles in one story. It's usually one story, one miracle. I believe this story was put in the Bible to show Jesus' peace when disruptions came. It's in numerous gospels, but we are going to look at the story in Mark 5:21–43.

Jesus had just departed from a boat and one of the rulers of the synagogue came and fell at his feet and begged Jesus to come and heal his daughter.

Jesus, full of compassion, went with him and crowds of people followed Him to see what He would do. With crowds like that, they must have been pressing up against Him, so many people at one stage or another along that journey were touching Him. But one touch came that stopped Jesus.

Jesus didn't brush off the touch as just one of the crowd. He knew that even though He was headed in one direction, there was a person there who had touched Him in a way nobody else had—by faith.

He stopped and asked the crowds, 'Who touched Me?' This was a weird question as there were multitudes touching Him but there was someone who had touched Him by faith and Jesus knew it was a woman (verse 32).

She responded to Jesus with her story—the whole truth of it, which probably took a long time. When I tell my husband a story, it takes a lot longer than if he tells me a story.

Jesus didn't rush her or tell her to hurry as He was on His way to Jairus' house. No, there was a peace around Jesus that surpassed all understanding. He had time for those who touched Him by faith.

Whilst she was telling her story, some people came and told Jairus his daughter had died. All seemed to be lost! But Jesus heard them and told Jairus to believe. Jesus wasn't concerned when He heard the news. He didn't get agitated and say, 'If only we'd gone there earlier.' He was totally at peace.

He then went and healed Jairus' daughter.

This story is helpful to remember when we get agitated and peace leaves us. Peace may leave us, but when we have the peace of Jesus that passes all understanding, which God promised to us, we can walk through our days being totally at peace, even in the midst of disruptions.

Disruptions may be God-appointed situations, so we shouldn't discount them.

Rest and peace are how we should be operating in our lives so before we end this chapter, let's pray:

*Father, we need your rest around our lives both in knowing that you are with us and in physical rest and sleep. Please help us to operate in both. We also speak over our lives that we have Your peace that passes all our understanding so that we continually walk in peace all day long. When disruptions come, please help us to discern whether they are from the enemy or are God-appointed situations in our lives. Thank you, God. In Jesus' name, amen.*

CHAPTER 13

# PLAN OF GOD

The plan of God feels like a scary set of words. What is the plan of God? Can we ever know the plan of God? What if I mess it up?

Joseph's story is a beautiful illustration of the plan of God for our lives. At the start of the story, Jacob and his family were living in their own land (not the Promised Land). When Joseph was sold into slavery to Egypt and then his family followed him there in a famine, it seems as if the plan of God to bring His children into the Promised Land was thwarted. Egypt seemed to be the wrong choice, or was it?

It looks like the wrong plan to us, but God has a way of navigating circumstances and situations into His perfect plan for our lives. The issue is that we forget or don't know what He has said in the past.

In Genesis 15, God showed Abram a vision and then made a covenant with him. The vision leads to the covenant.

In the covenant ceremony in verses 9 to 21, God makes this statement in verses 13 and 14:

> *Then He said to Abram: "Know certainly that your descendants will be strangers in a land that is not theirs, and will serve them, and they will afflict them four hundred years. And also, the nation whom they serve, I will judge; afterward they shall come out with great possessions..."*

Egypt was the place mentioned in this prophecy from God to Abram and that is where Abram's descendants now found themselves. It was no accident that they were there; it was the plan of God.

We know, however, that with God, the plan never goes from A to B to C. That's the same thing that happened with Abram's family.

God had to get Joseph into Egypt to enable the prophecy to be fulfilled but how was this going to happen?

Abraham and Sarah and their family travelled all over the place but there's no record of them ever going to Egypt. How was this to happen? Abraham and his family went where God directed them. It's not that they were disobedient, it's just that it wasn't time for them to arrive in Egypt yet.

This is the same for us. We receive a prophecy about something that will happen in our lives and we get all excited, thinking it's going to happen soon. But God's timing is not our timing, and we have to wait patiently and be obedient to the plan that God has for us right now.

Abraham's son Isaac grew up and was married to Rebekah. In Genesis 26, we read the story of there being a famine in the land. Look at what verse 2 and the beginning of verse 3 states:

> *Then the Lord appeared to him and said,*
> *"Do not go down to Egypt; live in the land of which*
> *I shall tell you. Dwell in this land..."*

God was very explicit in His instructions to Isaac. Even though there was a famine where he was living, he was not to go down to Egypt. It was not part of God's plan that Isaac go to the foreign land of Egypt either. It was not the right time. A famine eventually sent Jacob and his family to Egypt but only to buy grain, not to reside there.

Isaac had two sons—Esau and Jacob. Would one of them fulfil the promise God made to Abram a long time ago? Yes, they would—Jacob and his family would go to live in Egypt but only in difficult circumstances.

His son Joseph was sold to slave traders, and they took him to Egypt where, as can be seen earlier in this book, he became second in charge in Egypt. The family was finally fulfilling the plan of God from all those years ago.

The plan of God for your life and mine may come to pass in a very linear way but often it comes to pass as we try new things and walk around in circles for a while. But whilst the plan may take time, it will never be early and never be late. The only thing that can delay the plan of God for our lives is if we walk away from God or we don't allow Him to shape our character and handle our call.

Joseph knew of this prophecy because at the end of his life, he said these words in Genesis 50:24–25, in part:

> *"I am dying; but God will surely visit you and bring you out of this land to the land of which He swore to Abraham, Isaac, and to Jacob... God will surely visit you, and you shall carry my bones from here."*

Joseph knew of the plan of God that this wasn't Israel's final destination and as such, he wanted to be buried finally in the Promised Land.

Where God has each of us in life is in the place He wants us. We may have made choices that get us into bad situations but the town or place where you are living is where God wants you at this time. If He didn't, He would move you!

Proverbs 16:9 states:

> *A man's heart plans his way,*
> *But the Lord directs his steps.*

We might plan where we might live, the career we choose or who we marry, but the Lord directs the steps of those who are in tune with Him. Before we knew God, we might have made some bad choices but now that we are His, He can help us make good choices and direct our steps if we let Him.

There's a story like this in the life of Jesus (there are a few) where it looks like the plans were changed (especially to His disciples).

The first story is in John 4:3–4 and states:

> *He left Judea and departed again to Galilee. But He needed to go through Samaria.*

These two verses reveal a change of plans, but God was directing the steps of Jesus like He wants to do for us.

We can tell from the story of the Good Samaritan that Jews didn't really associate with Samaritans, so why did Jesus need to go through Samaria?

We find out a few verses later. A Samaritan woman and her town needed the ministry of Jesus. Therefore, Jesus was open to having his plans directed. By the time Jesus arrived there, it was noon, and he was weary, tired and thirsty. Jesus probably wondered why God had him at Jacob's well in the middle of the day. Nobody came to draw water then—the women came in the early morning and late afternoon when it was cooler.

However, in verse 7, a Samaritan woman comes to the well to draw water. This was why He was there, to minister into her life.

The woman and Jesus had a conversation and by the end of it, the whole town had come out to hear Him. He stayed an extra two days in that place because at that time it was God's plan for Him. His journey to Galilee could come later.

The other story in Jesus' life that I want to touch on is the death of Lazarus in John 11. Verses 3 and 6 state this:

> *Therefore, the sisters sent to Him, saying,*
> *"Lord, behold, he whom You love is sick"...*
> *So, when He heard that he was sick, He stayed two*
> *more days in the place where He was.*

What? Jesus stayed two more days instead of going to His friend at once? That sounds harsh and uncaring. The plans of God for our lives don't always make sense but they always bring God glory, if we obey them.

Further, there is a symbolic meaning in those two days that Jesus waited. It was to show us that 2000 years would pass before Jesus would come in the clouds to deliver the saints.

I wonder what Jesus did for those two days as the Bible doesn't tell us. Maybe He was pleading with God to release Him and let Him go to Lazarus or maybe He was just praying that God's will would be done in and through Him. Verse 4 is Jesus' faith statement for Lazarus:

> *"This sickness is not unto death, but for the glory of*
> *God, that the Son of God may be glorified through it."*

Jesus knew the Father's will for this circumstance. No matter what happened, Lazarus would live and God would be glorified.

The disciples were happy with the two-day wait as they were scared that Jesus was going to be killed if He went to Judea where Lazarus was (verses 8 and 16).

Although the plan was not what we would have wanted or what we would think that God would want, Jesus obeyed. He came to Bethany and was advised Lazarus had been dead for four days. This represents 4000 years of spiritual darkness before Jesus was born.

Instead of healing Lazarus, Jesus raised him from the dead. However, the lessons learned in this story and the glory God received from this story make the plan of God the right one.

Jesus was able to make His amazing statement in verses 25 and 26 that He wouldn't have been able to make if He'd just healed Lazarus. The statement is:

> *"I am the resurrection and the life. He who believes in Me, though he may die, he shall live. And whoever lives and believes in Me shall never die."*

Jesus was stating God's plan for mankind in these two sentences that may never have happened except for the delay in plans. If we believe in Jesus, we may die physically and then our bodies will be resurrected. Further, we won't die in our spirits or souls. They will live forever because we have been born again.

Jesus raised Lazarus from the dead and verse 45 tells of the results. Not only did Lazarus receive life and Mary and Martha receive their brother back, but many who had been there that day believed in Jesus. That's the greatest testimony and brings glory to God because only God can effect that sort of change in man.

Another person in the Bible who had to wait for God due to a change in plans was Paul.

Acts 16:6 is where the story starts and states:

> *Now when they had gone through Phrygia and the region of Galatia, they were forbidden by the Holy Spirit to preach the word in Asia. After they had come to Mysia, they tried to go into Bithynia, but the Spirit did not permit them. So, passing by Mysia, they came to Troas. And a vision appeared to Paul in the night. A man of Macedonia stood and pleaded with him, saying, "Come over to Macedonia and help us." Now after he had seen the vision, immediately we sought to go to Macedonia, concluding that the Lord had called us to preach the gospel to them.*

Does this feel like your life sometimes? It definitely can feel like mine! We feel that God wants us to do something but every direction we take is hindered and stopped. Most of the time we give up and lose heart, thinking to ourselves that God does not want to shift us from our current position.

Paul would have been a little frustrated too. It wasn't once that the Holy Spirit forbade them to go somewhere but twice in two verses. Granted, we don't know the period of time between these two verses, but it would have been frustrating nonetheless.

Did Paul give up? No, he kept moving forward one city at a time—from Phrygia through the region of Galatia to Mysia and then to Troas, where finally God spoke through a dream and told Paul the way to go.

The meaning of 'Phrygia' is 'dry' or 'barren'. The first place Paul started from was a dry, barren place. This is the place where our plans are stagnant and don't change much because it's not a place where plans are birthed.

He then went to Mysia, which means 'hidden' or 'covered'. This is a place we go through where the plans that God has for us are hidden or covered. They aren't hidden because God doesn't want us to see them, they're hidden so that our character can be built. This is a hidden place, sometimes known as a wilderness place, where plans for our lives are birthed in the spirit in a place where we can't see them (or we might run).

'Troas' means 'penetrated'. This is a place where the plans of God are entrenched in our lives, so we are ready to take the next steps with God. It's a place where we know the plans of God for us and have our character built enough to sustain those plans coming to fruition. This is where Paul had his dream and finally received a path forward.

The path can't be put into place in the lands of Phrygia or Mysia. If you find yourselves in those places, let God work His perfect will in you and don't be in too much of a hurry to travel through. Only move when its God's timing.

Paul kept moving but when he reached the place where God spoke to Him, everything else stopped.

What did Paul find in Macedonia? He found a woman named Lydia who opened her heart to the gospel, but the most exciting story was around the Philippian jailer being saved.

This story teaches us much about praise in hard places and words of knowledge but for Paul, it was much more. It was speaking the gospel in a new place and a book of the Bible being birthed from it. Both the books of Philippians and 1 and 2 Thessalonians were written to people in this region.

In my Bible, it states regarding the book of Philippians, that it was the most beautiful of Paul's letters, full of tenderness, warmth and affection. The dominant note throughout the letter is triumphant joy.

This book might never have been written if those other places had been available for Paul to preach in. God knows the exact plans and purposes for our lives and who will be impacted the most for the kingdom. This is the best way to live.

If we seek God for the plans He has for our lives, what are the verses in the Bible that we can gain insight from? My favourite one is Jeremiah 29:11, which has been quoted a few times throughout this book. It states:

> *For I know the thoughts that I think towards you,*
> *says the Lord, thoughts of peace and not of evil,*
> *to give you a future and a hope.*

If God is thinking about us, He's not only thinking about what a magnificent creation we are part of, but also of the plans He has for each member of that magnificent creation.

Another verse is 1 Timothy 4:14, which states:

> *Do not neglect the gift that is in you,*
> *which was given to you by prophecy,*
> *with the laying on of the hands of the eldership.*

This verse was written specifically to Timothy but as God is no respecter of persons, He has also given us a gift and a plan that we shouldn't neglect.

Hebrews 13:20–21 states:

> *Now may the God of peace who brought up our Lord*
> *Jesus from the dead, that great Shepherd of the sheep,*
> *through the blood of the everlasting covenant, make you*
> *complete in every good work to do His will, working in*
> *you what is well pleasing in His sight, through Jesus*
> *Christ to whom be glory forever and ever, Amen.*

Because of the work of Jesus on the cross and His resurrection, we have been given a good work to complete in our lives. This work is not done with our own abilities and talent but a work that is to do the will of God and to do that work in a way that is pleasing to God. God has a plan and purpose for us to do His will, not our own.

Sometimes our lives can take a certain direction, like being a policeman or doctor, but that may not be the will of God for our lives. It may be that's how we earn our living but God's plan for us may be teaching Sunday School or serving on the front door of the church. Whatever it is, it will bring God glory, even if we consider it small.

God doesn't have small and big gifts, He just has gifts and as long as we are obedient to Him, that's all that matters. If you do a jigsaw puzzle, some pieces may be smaller than others, but it doesn't mean they are less important. That small piece is needed just the same as the big piece if we are to complete the picture.

God is always concerned about the eternal picture and in that eternal picture, who was obedient to Him and who wasn't.

I will finish with this verse in Proverbs 3:5–6. It states:

> *Trust in the Lord with all your heart.*
> *And lean not on your own understanding.*
> *In all your ways acknowledge Him.*
> *And He shall direct your paths.*

Can you see the progression in these verses regarding the plan of God for your life?

Step 1 is to trust God with everything you have. This is the most important thing to do. If we don't trust God, we won't trust His plans for us, no matter how good they may be. We won't trust God's direction, timing or leading if we don't first and foremost trust Him.

Step 2 is don't lean on or rely on yourself. If we rely on ourselves, then we are going to make a mess of it. We will go down the 'shiny' path and not the right path. Human nature takes us down the easy path but that is not the path God wants us to take. Wide paths lead to destruction, narrow paths lead to God.

Step 3 is that we must acknowledge God. We must worship God and give Him glory in everything. Nothing good is done in our lives apart from God. Although God causes the rain to shine on the just and the unjust, it's still God who provides. Pray to God, worship God and stay in the presence of God.

Step 4 is the most exciting—God will direct our paths. Notice the word 'will'. It is not 'may' or 'could' but 'will'. This is crucial because sometimes we walk down a path that is unfamiliar or scary. If we know God is with us, we will walk down it unafraid and excited for the future. God only gives good gifts to His children, and He only has good plans for our lives.

Just as Joseph followed the plan of God for his life, may we allow God to direct us and follow the plan of God for our lives. It may be different from what we dreamed but it will always be better.

Let's pray:

> *Father, we trust You that You have a good plan for each of our lives, just like Joseph. This plan was put in place by you for our lives before the foundation of the world. It is a plan to fulfil your will for mankind and for your pleasure. Help us to just obey You and follow You wherever you lead. In Jesus' name, amen.*

CHAPTER 14

# ETERNAL PERSPECTIVE

As we have walked through Joseph's story from the prison to the palace, we can see the story unfolding for the children of Israel. Without the time living in Egypt, there never would have been a Moses to lead them out and stories of God's provision that provide glimpses of Who God is.

We sometimes consider our lives from an 80-year perspective, not realising that our story is part of a future generation's legacy.

Joseph left a legacy in Egypt for the children of Israel to follow. However, I want to have a look at what happened after he died. Did this legacy carry through to the next generation or did the influence of God's people in Egypt die with Joseph? What can we learn from what happened and how do we live our lives to ensure our legacy lives on?

Let's have a look at Genesis 50:22–26, which states:

> *So, Joseph dwelt in Egypt, he and his father's household. And Joseph lived one hundred and ten years. Joseph saw Ephraim's children to the third generation. The children of Machir, the son of Manasseh, were also brought up on Joseph's knees.*
>
> *And Joseph said to his brethren, "I am dying; but God will surely visit you and bring you out of this land to the land of which He swore to Abraham, Isaac, and to Jacob."*
>
> *Then Joseph took an oath from the children of Israel, saying, "God will surely visit you, and you shall carry up my bones **from** here." So, Joseph died, being one hundred and ten years old; and they embalmed him, and he was put in a coffin in Egypt.*

Joseph's last words to the children of Israel were legacy words. He gave them a promise that God would deliver them from the land of Egypt and give them the land that had been promised many generations before. As part of the faith of Joseph in this promise, he asked them to carry his bones and put them in that Promised Land.

Joseph didn't want his grave to be anywhere other than in the promises of God. How close must his relationship have been to God!

Those are the last words of the book of Genesis. Genesis starts with creation and leaves with a promise from God for

His people to continue believing His promises and living their lives accordingly. This is a word for each of us too. What God begins He finishes!

Now let's look at Exodus 1:6–8:

> *And Joseph died, all his brothers,*
> *and all that generation. But the children of Israel*
> *were fruitful and increased abundantly, multiplied and*
> *grew exceedingly mighty and the land was filled*
> *with them. Now there arose a new king over Egypt,*
> *who did not know Joseph.*

In these verses, don't you hear a 'but' coming? There's a change in that last verse. The children of Israel grew mighty, but a new king arose who didn't know the exploits of Joseph in the land. He was obviously not interested in who and what had gone before him but only cared about himself.

My question is (and I know the rest of the story), are the children of Israel going to rely on God in the times coming up and remember His promise or are they going to fall?

There are times in each of our lives when we are blessed exceedingly and everything goes along smoothly. But there will be one of those 'but' moments that come up for us.

For example:

1. A new company may take over our workplace
2. An illness may strike one of our family members

3. A new child may come into the area and our child becomes their friend and is led down a path that is not the way they should go
4. Our family needs to move town, state, etc., for some reason and we need to make new connections

Any one of these scenarios can make us forget the promises of God if we're not careful.

Is Joseph's legacy going to continue regarding trust in God through hard times or are the people so complacent that they won't even remember the things that he went through?

There are times in our lives when we need to forget the past, but there are also times when we need to be encouraged by the legacy of those who have gone before us. Before we look at that, let's look at the children of Israel's response.

This pharaoh was in such a state about the blessing of the children of Israel that he decided to make their lives bitter with hard bondage. However, they kept increasing, so then he decided to kill their baby boys. At this time, Moses was born, and we follow his story for 80 years.

In due course, God met Moses in the burning bush story in Exodus 3 and 4. God had seen the oppression of His people and had heard their cry. He had heard their weeping but not their faith in His promise.

I know that many times, I have cried out to God for healing, deliverance, an answer to prayer, etc., and God has heard my cry and answered. But how much better would it have been if I had just taken the promise of God and memorised it until it was hidden in my heart, knowing that God's promises all come true in due course? My countenance would not have been sorrowful but faithful and trusting.

There's a story in Luke 18 that puts this concept beautifully. It's the story of the persistent widow who begged the judge until she received what she wanted. However, in verse 8b, it states:

> *"...Nevertheless, when the Son of Man comes,*
> *will He really find faith on the earth?"*

This verse reminds me that it's better that I believe God's promises by faith than nag God in prayer until I receive what I want. Nagging doesn't produce trust in God, faith does.

At this point, we realise that the children of Israel had maybe forgotten the promise of God and were like the persistent widow in the story above.

Moses was sent back to Egypt to deliver the people out of the land (as Joseph had said many years before).

The first reaction to this news from the children of Israel is found in Exodus 4:31. It states:

> *So, the people believed; and when they heard*
> *that the Lord had visited the children of Israel and*
> *that He had looked on their affliction,*
> *then they bowed their heads and worshipped.*

Let's have a really good look at this verse:

1. They heard that God had visited the children of Israel. God doesn't visit—He is omnipresent. At this stage, He didn't live within them like He does with us today, but He definitely would have been there for them.
2. God looked on their affliction—what moved God for them was not faith but affliction. God was probably waiting for someone to rise up who would remember His promise but alas, nobody did. This is in contrast to Daniel in Daniel 9. When the 70 years of captivity had nearly ended, he started praying not whining.

   We need to remember this in our lives. God is looking for our faith in Him and His promises.
3. Only when they realised that God was now with them and had seen them did they bow their heads and worship. I wonder if the worship of God was part of their daily lives. Probably not.

   For you and me, it's essential that worship of God is part of our daily lives. It's not only singing slow songs but being conscious of God with us and depending on Him throughout the day that is our reasonable worship of God (Romans12:1).

Is this where the story ends? Not at all! Sometimes, in fact, most times, when God gives us a promise, we have to fight to get there. That fight is not against people but against the evil forces that are trying to prevent God's promise from coming to pass.

Moses went to Pharaoh in Exodus 5 to lay out the plan God had for His people. Do you think Pharaoh agreed with it? Of course not—the enemy will never agree with God's plans.

Pharaoh eventually complied with God's plans but only after 10 plagues had come and devastated the people.

More importantly for our chapter on legacy, we need to consider the further reactions of God's people. Did they stay on that promise from long ago that had been confirmed or did circumstances mess with their belief? Don't judge them—this can also happen to us.

After that first encounter with Pharaoh, Pharaoh made the people's tasks harder and really impossible. They not only had to make the desired quantities of brick but also collect their own building materials. This was an impossible situation.

Let's look at the Israelites' response to this news in verse 21. It states:

> *And they said to them, "Let the Lord look on you and judge, because you have made us abhorrent in the sight of Pharaoh and in the sight of his servants, to put a sword in their hand to kill us."*

What? Where was their belief in the promise now? They didn't even state the facts and then say, 'But God can deliver us.' There was no mention of God.

It's like when Jesus came into Jerusalem on Palm Sunday. The crowd rejoiced and called him Saviour but by Friday morning, they were screaming for him to be crucified.

There will always be a battle to fulfil the promise of God. That battle may be a sudden diagnosis, discouragement coming over your life or that all hell seems to break loose around you. But if you and I can encourage ourselves in those moments too, those things become just a show from the enemy like a fireworks show that makes a lot of noise but doesn't last long. The enemy can never defeat the Word of God unless we let him.

In Exodus 6, God again reminded the Israelites of His promise but in verse 9, it states they did not hear because of the anguish of their spirit and the cruel bondage. Sometimes we have to stand on the promises of God in spite of our feelings.

Finally, in Exodus 12:31, Pharaoh conceded and let the Israelites and all that belonged to them depart from the land of Egypt.

Before we leave this story, let's finalise Joseph's legacy and look at Exodus 13:19, which states:

> *And Moses took the bones of Joseph with him,*
> *for he had placed the children of Israel under solemn*
> *oath, saying, "God will surely visit you, and you shall*
> *carry up my bones from here with you."*

The legacy Joseph left them was now complete. His instructions at the end of his life were carried out.

Before we leave the chapter on legacy, I just want to have a look at another one.

Israel had settled in the Promised Land and then divided into two kingdoms, Judah and Israel. Israel had been taken into captivity and because of Judah not following God, they were about to be taken into captivity too. Unlike Israel, the people of Judah were given a timeframe of 70 years for their captivity.

When that time was drawing to a close, one man in the Bible, Daniel, sought God over that timeframe. The legacy of Judah was not to spend time in a foreign country under captivity but to again be settled in their own land.

Let's read the story in Daniel 9. Verses 1 to 3 states:

*In the first year of Darius the son of Ahasuerus, of the lineage of the Medes, who was made king over the realm of the Chaldeans – In the first year of his reign, I, Daniel understood by the books the number of the years specified by the word of the Lord through Jeremiah the prophet, that He would accomplish seventy years in the desolations of Jerusalem. Then I set my face toward the Lord God to make request by prayer and supplications, with fasting, sackcloth and ashes.*

Daniel realised that the legacy of time in a captive land was up so he did the only thing he knew—he prayed. But he didn't only pray, he confessed his sins and the sins of the nation in departing from God. What was the result? An angel came and advised him that his prayer had been heard and proceeded to give him a further vision of what was to take place after.

If you have read the story of the Jews returning to Jerusalem, you would realise that Daniel had no part in it. His part was to pray to open the door for the promise to be fulfilled and it was.

When you receive a promise and a legacy from God, make sure that you pray about it. God will hear you as He is a generational God. Stand on the promises He gives you and expect them to come to pass. God is not a liar but is the truth.

What legacy are you leaving your children and future generations? More importantly, are you pursuing your calling from God? That means your legacy will not only be about you and your family but will impact generations of others.

Let's pray:

*Father, we thank you for Joseph's legacy to the children of Israel. We pray that we will also leave a legacy, not only in our family but also for generations to come. Thank you, God, that you are always with us, and your promises will always come to pass if we believe. Amen.*

# EPILOGUE

As we have journeyed through this book from the prison to the palace of emotional healing, following the story of Joseph, we can be assured that God is with us through every journey in life that we undertake.

We can know that the promises of God are true and that He will never leave us or forsake us.

However, in the journey of life, our emotions will be battered occasionally by people or circumstances. It's up to us, however, to seek God for healing and perspective right at the start and not leave the emotions to become bigger than they should be.

Emotions are not bad. They are our guideposts to what is happening in our everyday world. We need to embrace them but not allow them to take over. Feelings will never go away but the sting of them will.

In my journey of emotional healing, I sometimes still feel rejected, but I have learnt to recognise it, process it and then take it to God. People can say things to us, but it's our response to them that makes all the difference. God is looking at our character development as it's in character development that He can move us further in our calling in Him.

I recently had a situation where my pastors cancelled a group I was leading. The group was only small but would have expanded over time. When I received the call, I was very hurt and felt a little rejected and that I wasn't doing a good job.

However, I had to pick myself up because it wasn't only my feelings that were going to be hurt, but others. I had to realise that God developing my character was more important than the group. God can raise up other similar groups in the church, but it was a test for me.

I realised that my response was going to make all the difference. A message needed to go out to the group, and some were upset. If I hadn't processed my response with God first, offence could have taken hold in not only my own life but in others.

I responded to the group in a way that was encouraging and uplifting, and gave them direction for where they were headed next. Since then, we have kept the group chat open and I still have great relationships with them, but I also carry no offence against the decision.

This is what each of us needs to do in relation to situations that arise. Process it yourself, go to God and let Him speak into your life. Sometimes you may need an impartial voice to speak into your life and that's okay.

I pray that this book has blessed you the way it has me as I was writing it. I pray that God has started to heal your deep hurts and that you will continue to work with God through it.

My greatest desire is that we are all healed emotionally and can live the life God intended for all of us, walking out the calling and purposes of God in our lives.

Let's pray:

*Father, I thank you that you have been with each and every one of us as we have journeyed through this book. I pray that You will continue what you started in each of our lives and bring us to that place of maturity in You where our lives can be an example to others. Thank you, God. Amen.*

# WANT TO KNOW JESUS

If you desire to have a relationship with Jesus, please pray this prayer:

Jesus, I come before you and repent of my sins. I believe that what Jesus did on the cross He did for me. I give you my life. Please help me to fulfil the plans and purposes You have for me. I want to live the life You intended for me.

In Jesus Name, Amen.

Congratulations you are now a child of God.

For further information, please contact me at

akroper@optusnet.com.au

I would love to hear from you!

## About the author

Karen is passionate about seeing people live their lives the way God intended and to fulfil the purpose and plans that God has for them.

She has run a number of life groups and taught teen church and Sunday school. She loves ministering to others one on one.

She resides in Australia with her husband and has two adult sons and three adult step daughters.

Continue your spiritual journey
**www.livingthelifegodintended.com**

www.ingramcontent.com/pod-product-compliance
Lightning Source LLC
Chambersburg PA
CBHW022055290426
44109CB00014B/1100